CORE SKILLS

Communication

FOR
Service
GNVQs

Health & Social Care
Hospitality & Catering
Leisure & Tourism

JOE HARKIN

Collins Educational
An imprint of HarperCollinsPublishers

Published in 1995 by Collins Educational
An imprint of HarperCollins*Publishers*
77–85 Fulham Palace Road
Hammersmith
London
W6 8JB

ISBN 0 00 320005 1

Design and typesetting by Derek Lee
Cover design by Derek Lee
Illustrated by Derek Lee and Harry Venning
Printed and bound by
Commissioning Editor Graham Bradbury
Project Editor Alison Walters

References

Grice, P. (1975) in P. Cole and J. Morgan (eds) *Syntax and Semantics, III: Speech Acts*, New York: Academic Press.

Gordon, S. (1912) *A Tramps's Sketches*.

Joyce, J. (1916) *Portrait of the Artist as a Young Man*, London: Jonathan Cape.

Keane, J. (1991) *The Media and Democracy*, Oxford: Polity Press.

Lakoff, R.C. (1977) 'The logic of politeness or minding your p's and q's', in A. K. Pugh, V. J. Lee and J. Swann (eds) *Language and Language Use*, Oxford: Heinemann.

Rodenburg, P. (1992) *The Right to Speak*, London: Methuen.

Tolkien, J. R. R. (1975) *Tree and Leaf*, London: Allen & Unwin.

Walker, J. (1995) *The Cost of Communication Breakdown*, London: Burston-Marsteller.

Acknowledgements

The publishers would like to thank 'Netley Waterside House', Winged Fellowship – Respite Care and Holidays for physically disabled people, for all their help in the research of this book.

Note from the author

The author would like to thank his students for what they have taught him; his wife and children, Rebecca, Danya and Joanne for their love and support; the designer, Derek Lee, and the illustrator, Harry Venning, for their flair and hard work; and the editors, Graham Bradbury and Alison Walters, for their commitment and enthusiasm.

CONTENTS

Introduction

Practice Activities

INTRODUCTION

This book is intended to develop the communication skills of learners taking GNVQs or NVQs in:

- Health & Social Care
- Hospitality & Catering
- Leisure & Tourism

How to use this book

Step 1: select the LEVEL of communication you wish to achieve (LEVEL 2 or LEVEL 3 – if you are uncertain, consult a *tutor*) and study the *Communication Specifications* (pages 6–13) to understand clearly which skills you need to practice and improve.

Step 2: turn to the *Practice Activities* to practise these skills. If you need help, turn to the *Help Section* at the back of the book.

Step 3: when you are ready, complete *assignments* (following the suggestions made in the *Evidence Opportunities* section and/or set on your GNVQ course) to produce evidence of achievement.

If you wish to be assessed, you should consult a tutor before or during the assignment work and read the complete Evidence Indicators given to you on your GNVQ course.

Step 4: once you have successfully completed an assignment, record your achievement using the tick-box system provided in the first section of this book, and on the forms provided on your GNVQ course.

Do you have a recognised learning difficulty?

If you have a difficulty (e.g. hearing, sight, speech, motor impairment) you may make use of any human, electronic or mechanical aids that you normally use when communicating. The National Council for Vocational Qualifications (NCVQ) states clearly that appropriate provision should be made for people who need to use:

- means of communication other than speech, including computers, technological aids, signing, symbols or lip reading;
- non-sighted methods of reading, such as Braille, or non-visual or non-aural ways of acquiring information;
- technological aids in practical and written work;
- aids of adapted equipment to allow access to practical activities.

If necessary, please consult your tutor in order to discuss your particular needs.

Suited to the audience and situation (PC2) at this level, the student should be able to vary and adapt contributions to take account of the audience, situation and purpose of the discussion and her/his role in it (e.g. deliberately using a variety of language to help others understand the points they are making; expressing points/ideas in different ways to assist others; using specialist vocabulary accurately; saying things clearly; contributing at appropriate points; taking account of the formality involved; using suitable tone, manner and gestures).

Confirm (PC3) actively checking understanding of key points to show that they have listened carefully and understood what has been said (e.g. asking questions to clarify points made by others, re-iterating accurately the points made by others).

Take forward the discussion (PC4) making contributions which build on the contributions of others and move the discussion on purposefully (e.g. asking follow-up questions, synthesising and summarising points made by others).

People who know the student (PC2 range) examples include other students, teachers, work colleagues, supervisors.

Level 2 Specification

Here are the specifications for Communication at level 2. Please also consult the core skills specifications you will have been given as part of your GNVQ course, and consult the person(s) who will assess you.

Element 2.1: Take part in discussions

PERFORMANCE CRITERIA

A student must:

PC1 make contributions which are relevant to the subject and purpose

PC2 make contributions in a way that is suited to the audience and situation

PC3 confirm that s/he has understood the contributions of others

PC4 make contributions which take forward the discussion

RANGE

Subject: straightforward

Purpose: to offer information, to obtain information, to exchange ideas

Audience: people familiar with the subject who know the student (A1), people familiar with the subject who do not know the student (A2)

Situation: one-to-one, group

Purpose (PC1) discussions in which the student has to give information to others, obtain information from others and exchange ideas. Discussions may allow students to demonstrate two or more of these purposes simultaneously (e.g. exchanging ideas with a graphic designer about how best to use colour and typeface to create a front cover for a promotional leaflet; presenting a care plan for a client and discussing the similarities and differences between the care plans for different client groups presented by other members of the group; getting information from a personnel manager about the process for recruiting trainee cashiers).

Straightforward (PC1 range) at this level, the student should be able to contribute to discussions on subjects which are routine and commonly occur in the settings in which s/he is working, using the appropriate vocabulary to convey information and ideas clearly. Examples of straightforward subjects include discussing the Health and Safety requirements which have to be observed in the workplace; discussing different methods used for testing and inspecting the quality of mass produced items leaving a production line.

People who do not know the student (PC2 range) examples include heads of department, students from different tutorial groups/courses or department, visitors, customers or clients

EVIDENCE INDICATORS

Tick and date the box(es) when you have achieved the following:

Subject+Audience	one-to-one discussions	group discussions
straightforward+A1 or A2	☐	☐
straightforward+A2	☐	☐

The four pieces of evidence should include:

• discussions with both audiences in range   A1 ☐   A2 ☐

Check text (PC2) involves making sure that it can be read easily and is complete (e.g. considering the clarity of handwriting, that all the details asked for have been included and, where IT is used, the spacing, typeface and type size are appropriate).

Purpose (PC4) written material produced for a purpose in the settings in which s/he is working (e.g. to give information, to obtain information, to express or find out opinions, to exchange ideas, to present an argument).

Straightforward (PC1 range) at this level, the student should be able to produce written materials on subjects which are routine and commonly occur in the settings in which s/he is working using the appropriate vocabulary to convey information and ideas clearly (e.g. schedules for other team members telling them about their responsibilities in a forthcoming event; a letter to a local business organisation requesting specific information about its activities).

People who know the student (PC4 range) examples include other students, teachers, work colleagues, supervisors.

Level 2 Specification

Element 2.2: Produce written material

PERFORMANCE CRITERIA

A student must:

PC1 include information which is accurate and relevant to the subject

PC2 check that text is legible and the meaning is clear, correcting it if necessary

PC3 follow appropriate standard conventions

PC4 present information in a format that suits the audience and purpose

PC5 use structure and style to emphasise meaning

RANGE

Subject: straightforward

Conventions: spelling, punctuation, grammar

Format: pre-set, outline

Audience: people familiar with the subject who know the student (A1), people familiar with subject who do not know the student (A2)

Standard conventions (PC3) spelling of words used regularly should be accurate (e.g. 'distillation', 'confidential', 'maintenance', 'aesthetic'). Dictionaries and spell-checkers can be used. Sentences should be complete, using a range of structures and appropriate punctuation (e.g. full stops, capital letters, commas, semi-colons, colons) in order to convey meaning clearly. Correct grammar should be used; for example, sentences with subject–verb agreement (e.g. using was/were correctly), relative clauses (e.g. using that/which correctly).

Structure and style (PC5) at this level, the student should be able to adapt the structure and style used appropriate to purpose to help the reader identify the main points and ideas (e.g. using paragraphs, sentences, headings and highlighting and specialist vocabulary precisely).

Pre-set formats (PC4 range) require information to be entered in clearly prescribed places with restricted space (e.g. record and report cards, application forms).

Outline formats (PC4 range) include those which have conventions in terms of layout and those where the structure is determined by others (e.g. business letters, reports where the order and/or length is prescribed, minutes or notes of a meeting).

People who do not know the student (PC4 range) examples include heads of department, those from a different tutorial group or department, visitors, customers, clients.

EVIDENCE INDICATORS

Tick and date the box(es) when you have achieved the following:

Subject+Audience	pre-set formats	outline formats
straightforward+A1 or A2	☐	☐
straightforward+A2	☐	☐

The four pieces of evidence should include:

- both audiences in range   A1 ☐   A2 ☐
- at least one hand-written piece   ☐

Images (PC1, PC2 and PC3) examples include maps, charts, tables, diagrams, sketches, photographs. The images selected may be reproduced or, where appropriate, cut out and used. IT could be used when students are producing their own images.

Use images (PC2 and PC3) the student should be able to use images to support the written and spoken communication s/he undertakes in the other elements at this level.

People who know the student (PC2 range) examples include members of a tutorial group, work colleagues, teachers, supervisors.

Purpose (PC2) the student should be able to use images when illustrating points s/he is making, in writing or in discussion, to help others understand the points (e.g. use two pie charts when explaining changes in the numbers employed in different industrial sectors between 1960 and 1990; include a diagram in a report to show how a pressure valve will operate when in use).

People who do not know the student (PC2 range) examples include heads of department, students from different tutorial groups/courses or department, visitors, customers or clients.

Level 2 Specification

Element 2.3:
Use images

PERFORMANCE CRITERIA
A student must:

PC1 select images which clearly illustrate the points being made

PC2 use images which are suited to the audience, situation and purpose

PC3 use images at appropriate times and places

RANGE

Images: taken from others' material, produced by the student

Points: on straightforward subjects

Audience: people familiar with the subject who know the student (A1); people familiar with the subject who do not know the student (A2)

Situation: in written material; in one-to-one discussions, in group discussions

EVIDENCE INDICATORS
Tick and date the box(es) when you have achieved the following:

Subject+Audience	one-to-one discussions	group discussions	written materials
straightforward+A1	☐	☐	☐
straightforward+A2	☐	☐	☐

The six pieces of evidence should include:
• images selected from others' material as well as produced by the student

Select materials (PC1) at this level, the student should identify potential materials which may contain the sort of information required and select those most appropriate for the purpose. Examples of materials include notices, letters, extracts from books or reports, newspaper or magazine articles, instruction leaflets, maps, charts, tables, diagrams, sketches, photographs.

Sources of reference (PC3) examples include using dictionaries to find meanings of words, using operating manuals to find out instructions, asking a work colleague for clarification.

Level 2 Specification

Element 2.4:
Read and respond to written materials

PERFORMANCE CRITERIA

A student must:

PC1 select and read materials for a purpose

PC2 extract the necessary information for a purpose

PC3 use appropriate sources of reference to clarify understanding of the subject

PC4 summarise the information extracted

RANGE

Materials: text, text supported by images, images supported by text

Purpose: to obtain information

Sources of reference: provided for the student; written, oral

Subject: straightforward

Summarise information: in writing, orally

Summarise information (PC4) involves identifying the main points from the extracted material and presenting them in a concise form. Students should be able to present summaries orally (e.g. in a short verbal report) as well as in writing (e.g. in a set of clearly structured notes).

Straightforward (PC3 range) at this level, the student should be able to read and respond to a range of material containing information and ideas expressed using the vocabulary which is commonly used in the settings in which s/he is working (e.g. a newspaper article outlining local objections to a new housing development, an extract from a magazine article describing the work of an artist, an extract from a book describing changing trends in numbers employed in part-time and full-time jobs).

Purpose (PC1 and PC2) the student should obtain the necessary information from written materials (e.g. get instructions, directions, facts, opinions or ideas). The student should be able to identify and understand key points/ideas and extract the meaning accurately.

EVIDENCE INDICATORS
Tick and date the box(es) when you have achieved the following:

Subject	text	text supported by images	images supported by text
straightforward	☐	☐	☐
straightforward	☐	☐	☐

The six pieces of evidence should include:
• a record of the purpose for reading the material
• a statement of the oral and written sources of reference used to clarify understanding
• at least two oral and two written summaries of information extracted from the materials read

Suited to the audience and situation (PC2) at this level, the student should be able to vary and adapt contributions to take account of the audience, situation and purpose of the discussion and their role in it, choosing how and when to participate (e.g. using vocabulary precisely and organising contributions to match the demands of the situation; using a variety of language and suitable markers to help others understand the point the student is making; saying things clearly; contributing at appropriate points; taking account of the formality involved; using suitable tone, manner and gestures.

Confirm (PC3) actively checking understanding of key points to show that they have listened carefully and understood what has been said (e.g. asking questions to clarify points made by others, re-iterating accurately the points made by others).

Take forward the discussion (PC4) making contributions which build on the contributions of others' and move the discussion on purposefully (e.g. asking follow-up questions, synthesising and summarizing points made by others).

Create opportunities for others to contribute (PC5) examples include: inviting others to contribute; encouraging others known to have alternative views/additional information to contribute; expressing views which provoke responses; encouraging others to develop points they have made or re-state them in different ways to help their own and other group members' understanding.

People who know the student (PC2 range) examples include other students, teachers, work colleagues, supervisors.

Level 3 Specification

Here are the specifications for Communication at level 3. Please also consult the core skills specifications you will have been given as part of your GNVQ course, and consult the person(s) who will assess you.

Element 3.1: Take part in discussions

PERFORMANCE CRITERIA

A student must:

PC1 make contributions which are relevant to the subject and purpose

PC2 make contributions in a way that is suited to the audience and situation

PC3 confirm that s/he has understood the contributions of others

PC4 make contributions which take forward the discussion

PC5 create opportunities for others to contribute

RANGE

Subject: straightforward, complex

Purpose: to offer information, to obtain information, to exchange ideas

Audience: people familiar with the subject who know the student (A1), people familiar with the subject who do not know the student (A2); people not familiar with the subject who know the student (A3), people not familiar with the subject who do not know the student (A4)

Situation: one-to-one, group

Purpose (PC1) discussions in which the student has to give information to others, obtain information from other people and exchange ideas. Discussion may allow students to demonstrate two or more of these purposes simultaneously (e.g. giving information to customers about the range of sports facilities available in a leisure centre; exchanging information about the different ways local employers ask job applicants to present personal information; obtaining information from a local architect how he tackled a design brief for new accommodation for a local surgery/GP practice).

Straightforward (PC1 range) at this level, the student should be able to contribute to discussions on subjects which are routine and commonly occur in the settings in which s/he is working, using the appropriate vocabulary to convey information and ideas clearly. Examples of straightforward subjects include discussing with clients the packaging and labeling requirements for delicate mass-produced items which will be transported in different ways; discussing with other team members the contingency arrangements which might be needed if bad weather affects a social event which cannot be rescheduled.

Complex (PC1 range) at this level, the student should also be able to deal with more complex subjects, for example complicated reasoning, sensitive issues or the interpretation of others' points of view. This will require careful choice of vocabulary and structuring of what is said. The student should use specialist terms appropriately and vary the way s/he expresses things in order to help other people understand (e.g. reporting to other students about how the local forestry commission tries to balance environmental considerations with increasing demands from the public for access to beauty spots; finding out about different ways of alerting young people to the dangers of alcohol abuse from a counsellor who deals with alcohol-related problems; exchanging ideas with an advertising executive about the design of a promotional campaign aimed at a particular market segment).

People who do not know the student (PC2 range) examples include heads of department, those from a different tutorial group or department, visitors, customers, clients.

EVIDENCE INDICATORS

Tick and date the box(es) when you have achieved the following:

Audience	one-to-one discussions	group discussions
A4	☐	☐
A4	☐	☐
	☐	☐
	☐	☐

The eight pieces of evidence should include:

- both straightforward and complex subjects
- discussions with all audiences in range   A1 ☐   A2 ☐   A3 ☐   A4 ☐

Check text (PC2) involves making sure that it can be read easily and is complete (e.g. considering the clarity of handwriting, that all the details asked for have been included and, where IT is used, the spacing, typeface and type size are appropriate).

Standard conventions (PC3) spelling of words used regularly in the settings in which s/he is working should be accurate (e.g. 'psychological', 'confidentiality', 'representation'). Dictionaries and spell-checkers can be used. Sentences should be complete, using a range of structures and appropriate punctuation (e.g. capital letters, full stops, apostrophes, inverted commas, brackets, hyphens) in order to convey meaning clearly. Correct grammar should be used; for example, sentences with subject–verb agreement (using was/were correctly), relative clauses (using that/which correctly).

Pre-set formats (PC4 range) include those requiring information to be entered in clearly prescribed places with restricted space, for example application forms, record and report cards.

Outline formats (PC4 range) include those which have conventions in terms of layout and those where the structure is determined by others (e.g. business letters, reports where the order and/or length is prescribed, minutes or notes of a meeting).

Freely structured formats (PC4 range) are those where the student determines how to organise and present written material appropriate for the purpose and audience (e.g. a brochure to encourage healthy eating by elderly people, a report for a marketing manager describing the performance of a leisure facility which includes recommendations on how to improve take-up by local teenagers).

People who know the student (PC4 range) examples include other students, teachers, work colleagues, supervisors.

Level 3 Specification

Element 3.2: Produce written material

PERFORMANCE CRITERIA

A student must:

PC1 include information which is accurate and relevant to the subject

PC2 check that text is legible and the meaning is clear, correcting it if necessary

PC3 follow appropriate standard conventions

PC4 present information in a format that suits the audience and purpose

PC5 use structure and style to emphasise meaning

RANGE

Subject: straightforward, complex

Conventions: spelling, punctuation, grammar

Format: pre-set, outline, freely structured

Audience: people familiar with the subject who know the student (A1), people familiar with the subject who do not know the student (A2); people unfamiliar with the subject who know the student (A3), people unfamiliar with the subject who do not know the student (A4)

Purpose (PC4) written material produced for a purpose in the settings in which s/he is working (e.g. to give information, to obtain information, to express or find out opinions, to exchange ideas, to present an argument).

Structure and style (PC5) at this level, students should produce material which requires varied choice of vocabulary and careful structuring of what is written to make the sequence of events and the main ideas coherent and clear to the reader (e.g. in terms of sentence structure, using paragraphs, headings, sub-headings, indentation and highlighting).

Straightforward (PC1 range) at this level, the student should be able to produce written materials on subjects which are routine and commonly occur in the settings in which s/he is working, using the appropriate vocabulary to convey information and ideas clearly. Examples of straightforward subjects include a set of instructions for others on how and when to use a particular first aid technique, a report which compares the performance of particular UK industrial sectors with those in other countries in the EU.

Complex (PC1 range) at this level, the student should also be able to deal with more complex subjects, for example complicated reasoning, sensitive issues or the interpretation of others' point of view. This will require careful use of specialist vocabulary and careful structuring of what is written in order to convey events and ideas clearly to the reader (e.g. a report of a site visit describing work in progress which analyses the causes and effects of delay in the availability of particular skilled labour, a report of an interview with a GP fund-holder which indicates the advantages and disadvantages the doctor believes the status gives her compared to the previous arrangements).

People who do not know the student (PC4 range) examples include heads of department, those from a different tutorial group or department, visitors, customers, clients.

EVIDENCE INDICATORS

Tick and date the box(es) when you have achieved the following:

pre-set formats   **outline formats**   **freely-structured formats**

☐   ☐   ☐
☐
☐
☐

The six pieces of evidence should include:
- at least four pieces on complex subjects   ☐   ☐   ☐   ☐
- all four audiences in range   A1 ☐   A2 ☐   A3 ☐   A4 ☐
- at least one hand-written piece   ☐

Images (PC1, PC2 and PC3) examples include maps, charts, tables, diagrams, sketches, photographs. The images selected may be reproduced or, where appropriate, cut out and used. IT could be used when students are producing their own images.

Purpose (PC2) the student should be able to use images when illustrating points they are making, in writing or in discussion, to help others understand the points (e.g. using an organisation chart showing lines of responsibility for different care services within a local Health Authority when presenting findings of a project).

Level 3 Specification

Element 3.3: Use images

PERFORMANCE CRITERIA

A student must:

PC1 select images which clearly illustrate the points being made

PC2 use images which are suited to the audience, situation and purpose

PC3 use images at appropriate times and places

RANGE

Images: taken from others' material, produced by the student

Points: on straightforward subjects, on complex subjects

Audience: people familiar with the subject who know the student (A1), people familiar with the subject who do not know the student (A2); people not familiar with the subject who know the student (A3), people not familiar with the subject who do not know the student (A4)

Situation: in written material; in one-to-one discussions, in group discussions

Use images (PC2 and PC3) the student should be able to use images to support the written and spoken communication s/he undertakes in the other elements at this level.

People who know the student (PC2 range) examples include other students, teachers, work colleagues, supervisors.

People who do not know the student (PC2 range) examples include heads of department, students from different tutorial groups/courses or department, visitors, customers or clients.

EVIDENCE INDICATORS

Tick and date the box(es) when you have achieved the following:

Subject+Audience	one-to-one discussions	group discussions	written materials
complex+A4	☐	☐	☐
complex	☐	☐	☐
			☐
			☐

The eight pieces of evidence should include:

- all four audiences for written materials   A1 ☐   A2 ☐   A3 ☐   A4 ☐
- images selected from others' material as well as produced by the student

Select materials (PC1) at this level, the students is able to identify potential materials which may contain the sort of information most appropriate for the purpose (e.g. ensuring the materials contain all of the information necessary for the purpose in hand, are up-to-date if this affects relevance, are appropriate in terms of containing the fact and/or opinion required). This may involve using skills such as scanning to get an overview of the structure and content and skim-reading to identify the main points. Examples of materials include notices, letters, extracts from books and reports, newspaper and magazine articles, instruction leaflets, maps, charts, tables, diagrams, sketches, photographs.

Purpose (PC1 and PC2) the student should be able to obtain the necessary information from written materials (e.g. get instructions, directions, facts, opinions or ideas). The student should be able to identify and understand key points/ideas and extract the meaning accurately.

Sources of reference (PC3) examples include using dictionaries to find meanings of words, asking a work colleague for clarification.

Level 3 Specification

Element 3.4: Read and respond to written materials

PERFORMANCE CRITERIA

A student must:

PC1 select and read materials for a purpose

PC2 extract the necessary information for a purpose

PC3 use appropriate sources of reference to clarify understanding of the subject

PC4 summarise the information extracted

RANGE

Materials: text, text supported by images, images supported by text

Purpose: to obtain information

Sources of reference: provided for the student, sought out by the student; written, oral

Subject: straightforward, complex

Summarise the information: in writing, orally

Summarise information (PC4) involves identifying the main points from the extracted material and presenting them in a concise form. Students should be able to present summaries orally (e.g. in a short verbal report) as well as in writing (e.g. in a set of clearly structured notes).

Straightforward (PC3 range) at this level, the student should be able to read and respond to material containing information and ideas expressed using the vocabulary which is commonly used in the settings in which s/he is working (e.g. a design brief for a fire resistant package, including drawings and descriptions of materials and processing required for a small batch production; a chapter describing the ways in which different management structures are typically found in different size businesses).

Complex (PC3 range) at this level, the student should be able to read and respond to materials which involve responding to more complex subjects, such as complicated lines of reasoning, sensitive issues or the interpretation of others' points of view. This may require an understanding of specialist vocabulary, the capacity to follow complex trains of thought and to form accurate judgments (e.g. a technical description in a journal of the development of a portable product for purifying large quantities of salt water rapidly; a brochure comparing the strengths and weaknesses of a range of graphics packages; a case history of an elderly patient who, despite increasing immobility, is supported by various local care services and, as a result, is able to continue living in her own home).

EVIDENCE INDICATORS
Tick and date the box(es) when you have achieved the following:

Subject	text	text supported by images	images supported by text
straightforward	☐	☐	☐
straightforward	☐	☐	☐
complex	☐	☐	☐
complex	☐	☐	☐

The twelve pieces of evidence should include:
• a record of the purpose for reading the material
• a statement of the oral and written sources of reference used to clarify understanding
• at least two oral and two written summaries of information on complex subjects extracted from the materials read

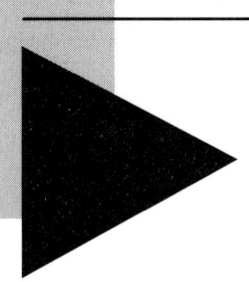

PRACTICE ACTIVITIES

The setting

Freedom Holidays is an organisation, run by paid staff and unpaid volunteers, dedicated to providing relaxing holidays for people with physical disabilities.

It has a number of centres around the country, each in a beautiful location. The centre chosen for these practice activities is Francis House, which is situated by the sea and close to a large town.

Francis House has 16 single bedrooms and 5 double bedrooms, each with a private bathroom and views over the gardens to the sea. It is run by a small team of dedicated people:

- care staff: nurses and auxiliaries
- domestic staff: caterers and housekeepers
- entertainments staff

Guests going on a Freedom Holiday do not pay the full price – the difference is made up by donations from companies and individuals, and by fund-raising events.

The volunteers who staff the centres spend one or two weeks working closely with the guests – they are the arms, legs, companions and friends of the guests, and also help the domestic and kitchen staff.

Francis House provides the following facilities:

- wheelchair access to all rooms
- 24-hour nursing and volunteer support
- indoor heated swimming pool
- organised trips and outings
- television lounge
- attractive licensed bar
- craft/activities room
- personal help call buttons in every room

The activities and outings include:

- sightseeing minibus tours
- sports: swimming, pony riding
- trips: theatre, shopping
- indoor fun: games, discos

Special interest holidays are organised for people who love Drama, Photography, Painting, Birdwatching, Music, Crafts, Cricket and Fishing. Special weeks are also arranged for children.

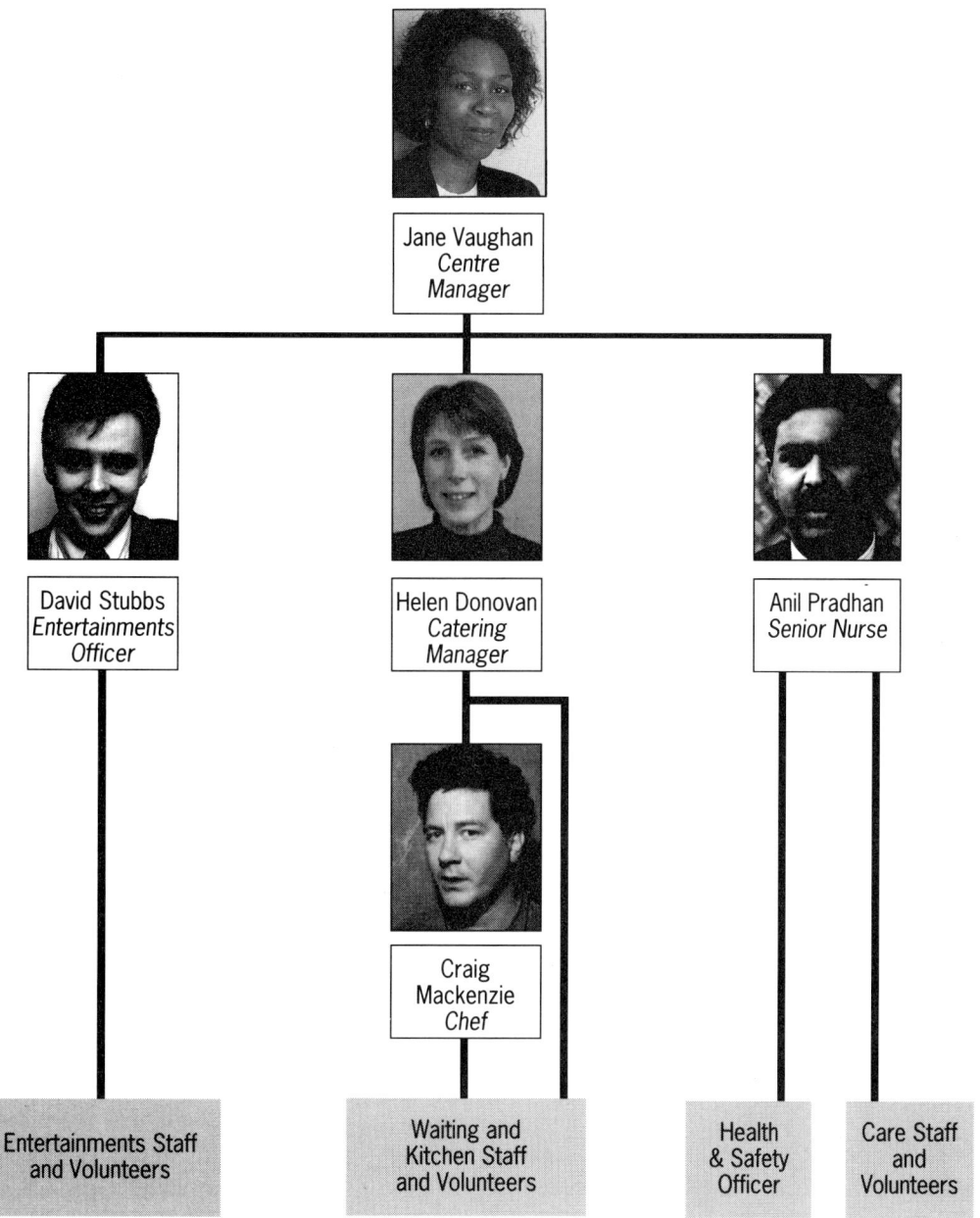

The attitude of the staff is crucial. All people, including those with physical disabilities, need dignity and respect. Staff and volunteers try at all times to show the right attitude to guests. They must be helpful and efficient because guests are paying for a holiday and have the right to high standards of service; they must be cheerful and friendly to make the guests' stay as happy as possible; and, above all, they must not patronise or talk down to guests because they are physically disabled.

Teamwork is essential because looking after disabled people can be physically and emotionally demanding.

The practice activities that follow (pages 16–74) are based on the work that staff and volunteers carry out at Francis House.

1   Management responsibilities

The Centre Manager at Francis house, Jane Vaughan, has to employ a wide range of communication skills that include:

- ▶ encouraging and advising staff and volunteers
- ▶ responding to telephone enquiries
- ▶ making oral presentations to staff and guests
- ▶ writing a wide variety of documents, from standard forms and letters, to magazine articles
- ▶ producing images to illustrate points made in presentations
- ▶ reading and responding to a wide variety of documents

The organisation chart

Jane Vaughan decides to draw up a simple organisation chart, showing the key permanent staff of Francis House. The chart will enable volunteers and guests to know who is who more quickly.

Guidance

An organisation chart is an example of a flow diagram. Flow diagrams show the connections between different elements by means of lines, arrows, etc. They should be easy to read at a glance.

Using images: still photographs of staff

When people are in one another's company for only a few days, it is sometimes difficult for them to recall each other's names. To help guests and volunteers recognise and get to know who is who among the permanent staff, Jane decides to have staff photographs taken and displayed with the organisation chart, on a notice board at a height suitable for all (including wheelchair users) to see.

Guidance

Photographs are a powerful way of illustrating points when you are speaking and writing. Imagine how much less of an impact newspapers would have if they did not use photographs to illustrate news items. Think about advertising material too, and how it so often relies almost entirely on visual images to convey a message.

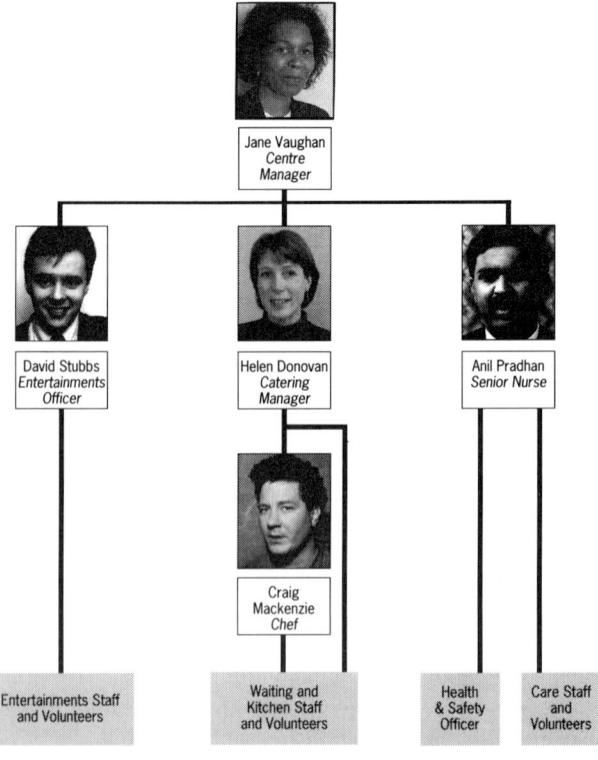

Whether a photograph or other image is at LEVEL 2 or LEVEL 3 within USE IMAGES depends on the *context* in which it is used. If it is used to support complex, non-routine communication, then it is likely to be LEVEL 3.

Using photos in an organisational chart is at LEVEL 2, because displaying photos of staff is routine in many organisations; and guests will be used to seeing photos of other people.

 PRACTICE

CONSIDER whether there are opportunities for you to make greater use of photographs, or other images, to help communicate information.

? HELP
If you need help to use images, turn to page 117.

 **EVIDENCE**
Assignment 15 (page 79) provides an opportunity to produce evidence of achievement in using photographs.

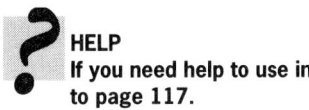
The article for a leisure magazine

Guidance

The article is non-routine and is written for people who will be unfamiliar with the subject matter, therefore it meets the requirements of PRODUCE WRITTEN MATERIAL at LEVEL 3. The information it contains is accurate and relevant (PC1); it is legible to the magazine editor (PC2); it is written in English that follows standard conventions (PC3); it is organised in a freely structured format that suits the subject (PC4); and it uses structure and style, through choice of vocabulary and paragraphing, to emphasise meaning and help the reader (PC5).

The Editor of a leisure magazine telephones Jane Vaughan to ask if she will submit a brief article about Freedom Holidays. The Editor suggests that the article should be 'chatty and anecdotal, without too many facts and figures'. She asks if Jane can also send some photographs of the Centre that would be suitable to illustrate the article.

As is usual with writing that is not routine, Jane makes some notes and drafts a first attempt. She does not expect to be able to produce a suitable article without re-drafting and polishing.

Here are her notes:

> Situation of Francis House
> View from the windows
> Staff characters
> New volunteers each week
> The arrival of guests
> The purpose of Francis House
> The desired atmosphere at Francis House
> Funny incidents
> Accidents
> Getting out and about
> The end of the holiday: tears and farewells
> Another batch of volunteers arrive

These notes help Jane to gather her thoughts. She will not necessarily deal with all these ideas, nor in the order that she has written them; and other ideas may occur to her as she writes.

Guidance

All writers need to draft and re-write, especially if the subject is complex, or if the audience knows little or nothing about the subject. Re-drafting is not a sign of weakness as a writer – it is often quite the reverse.

Having gathered her thoughts, Jane attempts a first draft which she then reads through and changes where she thinks it is necessary. Here is the first part of it:

A Freedom Holiday gives disabled people ~~the~~ *an* opportunity to get away from their usual surroundings for a week or two, while being looked after properly by skilled staff. It also gives their regular carers a ~~break so that they can re-charge their batteries~~ *well-earned rest.*

There is a charge but ~~it~~ *this* is lower than the costs and no one is refused a holiday because they can't afford it. The excess is met by ~~contributions~~ *donations*, and costs are kept down by employing unpaid volunteers.

~~Helpers~~ *Volunteers* from the local community, and from all over the country and even overseas, help to make guests' stay as relaxing and enjoyable as possible.

From the window of each guest bedroom there is a view of ~~When a guest looks out of the window of their bedroom they see~~ the sea. At times the water sparkles in the sun~~light~~ or moonlight; at other times it is grey and wild with spray reaching the buildings, flecking the window panes with salt.

Great emphasis is put on staff being efficient and caring, *The most important factor in making a holiday remarkable is staff attitudes.* and at the same time cheerful and friendly. Years after *their stay at Francis House* ~~Freedom holiday~~, we want guests to be able to *smile when they remember the holiday because of the genuine warmth of the* ~~close their eyes and recall the happy faces of our~~ staff and volunteers and their hard work to ensure that people have an enjoyable time.

Each week new volunteers arrive. They ~~often look~~ *come in* all shapes, sizes and ages, ~~from~~ sixteen ~~year old college students~~ to sixty ~~year-olds~~, male and female, black and white, they are a cross-section of the population. Some swagger in with a broad grin to hide their apprehension; others look around nervously, wondering if they will cope. They nearly all do. Very few volunteers pack their bags and take the next train home.

Notice that Jane has not been able to include all her ideas in the article, as that would make it too long. She has had to select those ideas that she thinks will be most interesting to the reader. This is common when writing.

Using images: photographs

Jane selects a suitable photograph of Francis House to accompany the article. It is a picture of the staff and some volunteers with a group of guests enjoying themselves on holiday at Francis House.

Choosing a photo will be at LEVEL 3 because it is going to be used in a LEVEL 3 context – an article about complex subject matter; for an audience unfamiliar with the subject.

 **PRACTICE**

USE any opportunity that arises to work on an extended piece of writing. It does not have to be an article for a paper. It could be an essay, or a report. Bear in mind the needs of the audience. Ensure that you deal with important information in the opening paragraphs so that the reader is introduced to the subject logically. Be prepared to make preliminary notes and to re-draft and polish your writing to make it as informative and readable as possible.

Consider whether you should use images to illustrate your article.

 HELP
If you need help with any aspect of writing, turn to page 97.

 **EVIDENCE**
Assignment 14 (page 79) provides an opportunity to produce evidence of achievement in writing an article.

Reading the article: identifying unfamiliar words

You may have found words that are unfamiliar or that you don't fully understand in the article above. Very often you can guess the meaning from the *context* – the rest of the sentence (or other sentences in the paragraph) gives clues to meaning. Sometimes it is necessary to look up a word in a dictionary or other reference book.

Consider the word 'apprehension' in the final paragraph of the article: 'Some [volunteers] swagger in with a broad grin to hide their apprehension'. A reader uncertain about the meaning of the word could look it up in a dictionary, where they would learn that 'apprehension' is a noun with several possible meanings: arrest; grasping of ideas; dread. The definition that fits the meaning of 'apprehension' in the article depends on context. Look again at the last paragraph – no one is being arrested; there is no reason why volunteers would wish to hide their grasping of ideas; so the appropriate meaning is 'dread'. But does this fit accurately? Would a volunteer really dread the prospect of working at Francis House?

A reader, or writer, unsure about the appropriateness of 'dread' could look up the word in a thesaurus, where alternative words such as 'fright', 'horror', 'terror', 'trepidation', 'anxiety' and 'uneasiness' will be listed, along with 'apprehension'. Which word do you think most closely matches the feeling of a new volunteer entering Francis House for the first time?

The truth is that some will feel terror, and others only uneasiness; hence a more general word, 'apprehension', has been used by the writer to include all possible degrees of anxiety.

> ### Guidance
>
> English is a very rich and complex language, with many alternative words to express fine shades of meaning. The use of a dictionary and a thesaurus can help you to use language with precision.

PRACTICE

M AKE use of a dictionary and/or a thesaurus to help you identify words with which you are not fully familiar.

 HELP
If you need help with using a dictionary or a thesaurus, turn to page 125.

 **EVIDENCE**
Assignment 21 (page 80) provides an opportunity of producing evidence of attainment in this skill.

Guidance

The points in the article are made in a logical order of importance. People need to know what Freedom Holidays are before learning about costs; it is more important for them to know that costs are kept low before reading about volunteers.

Reading the article: summarising the main points

Read the first two paragraphs of Jane's article (p.20). How many 'main points' can you identify?

There are four, although some may be sub-divided:

Disabled people can have a holiday in safe hands (paragraph 1)
Their carers can have a rest (paragraph 1)
There is a charge but (paragraph 2):
it is lower than costs
no one is turned away
The extra costs arc mct by (paragraph 2):
donations
employing volunteers

 PRACTICE

W HEN you read an article or report, notice how the writer introduces main points in the opening paragraphs, and builds on these in a logical way. Try to do the same in your own writing.
   If you wish to summarise the main points, make some structured notes, as in this example.

 HELP
If you need help in reading effectively, turn to page 123.

 **EVIDENCE**
Assignment 21 (page 80) provides an opportunity to produce evidence of achievement in using sources of reference.

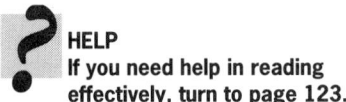 **A notice for new guests**

Guidance

A logo is an image used as the badge of an organisation. It should be eye catching, so that people come to associate the organisation with the logo.

Most guests arrive at Francis House on a Saturday afternoon and it is not always possible for the Centre Manager to greet them personally. In order to help make them feel welcome, she prepares a simple notice to be handed to each of them.

Using images: a logo

In order to give the notice more impact and to give the reader a clearer image of Francis House, Jane Vaughan decides to illustrate the notice with a logo that will show the spirit of Francis House, as 'fun with care'.

Many logos are produced by professional designers, but this would be too expensive for Francis House, so Jane decides to design a simple logo herself. Here is the notice and the logo she has designed:

FRANCIS HOUSE

Welcome from the staff and volunteer team at Francis House. We hope you will enjoy your holiday with us. Should there be anything we can do to improve it or to make your stay even more memorable please tell us and we will endeavour to do our very best to help.

▶ PRACTICE

USE any opportunity that presents itself to prepare a notice. Ensure that it meets all the criteria for PRODUCE WRITTEN MATERIAL and pay particular attention to the size of lettering, the layout and whether you should use an image to illustrate it.

HELP
If you need help in producing written material, turn to page 97.

EVIDENCE
Assignment 16 (page 79) provides an opportunity to produce evidence of achievement in producing a poster or notice.

Greeting guests

When she can, Jane Vaughan likes to greet each guest personally. She is not able to talk to them for long but feels it is important to make them feel welcome. For her this is a routine part of her work (LEVEL 2).

Jane always aims to discuss non-threatening subjects that the guest will know about, e.g. the weather, the guest's journey, whether they have visited the area before (PC1). She will speak clearly, in a suitable tone and manner (PC2); will listen attentively to what the guest has to say (PC3); and will ask questions and make other contributions to take forward the discussion (PC4).

▶ PRACTICE

MAKE a recording (preferably on video) of routine conversations, both genuine and role-play, with other people (friends, customers, tutors). Try to make these as natural as possible. What can you learn about your tone and manner in speaking and listening?

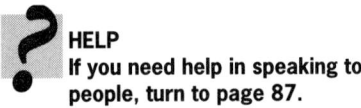

HELP
If you need help in speaking to people, turn to page 87.

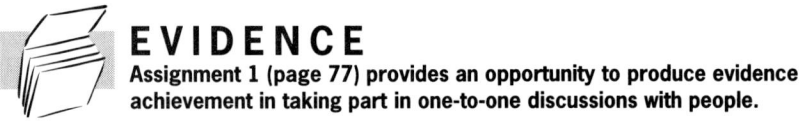

E V I D E N C E
Assignment 1 (page 77) provides an opportunity to produce evidence of achievement in taking part in one-to-one discussions with people.

Talking to new volunteer helpers

Guidance

People cannot take in lots of new information in a short time, especially if they are in unfamiliar surroundings. For presentations it is always necessary to make conscious choices about what to focus on, based on factors such as what people may know already, and how alert they may be.

Each week new volunteers arrive from all over the country, and sometimes from abroad, to spend a week or two working at Francis House. Jane Vaughan always gives a short presentation in which she welcomes them and introduces them to their work at the Centre.

Here is a list of topics Jane could cover, from which she will select those she thinks most important:

Hello and general welcome to Francis House
Introduce staff – colour badge system
Use of lifts
Smoking areas
TV lounges
Money, valuables, etc.
Bar, shop, opening hours
Meal times; visitors' meals
Serving of meals – volunteers' roles
Call system demonstration
Outings/entertainments; display boards; booking system
Local area – gardens, beach, sights, etc.
Fire procedures
Pay phones
Laundry system
Hairdresser
Chiropodist
Sports facilities
Helping guests to bath and dress
Talking to guests
Helping the staff
Role of local volunteers – serving breakfast; helping on trips, etc.

As you can see, to talk about each of these topics would take too long, even if the volunteers could take them all in. So Jane selects, for example:

* Welcome to Francis House and thanks for volunteering
* Introduce key members of staff
* Helping the staff – emergency procedures
* The ethos of the Centre – holiday with care
  ○ importance of speaking and listening to guests
* Admission routine

She decides that all other topics will have to be dealt with in a booklet, or will have to wait.

Having chosen what to talk about, Jane's next task is to decide how the topics should be presented. The points she takes into account fulfil all the Performance Criteria for TAKE PART IN DISCUSSIONS at LEVEL 3. She will try to:

Guidance

Jane's presentation is at LEVEL 3 because it is designed to give information to people who may have little knowledge of the subject matter; and it is also complex information.

Guidance

Prepare carefully for presentations but do not over-prepare so that you become stale. If in doubt, try it on a friend first. Use notes to jog your memory but never read aloud for more than a few moments because this can be very tedious for an audience.

- keep to the purpose of the presentation (PC1);
- speak in a tone and manner suited to the audience and situation (PC2);
- listen attentively to any contributions from the audience and show that she has understood (PC3);
- ask questions or summarise points to take forward the discussion (PC4);
- invite volunteers to ask questions (PC5).

In preparation for her presentation, Jane may make a few brief notes to jog her memory about what she wishes to say, but she will avoid reading from them directly because reading aloud from a prepared script for more than a few moments can be very tedious for an audience. Instead, she will occasionally glance at them so that she does not lose her thread.

Using images: sketches

To make her presentation more interesting, Jane Vaughan decides to draw a few simple cartoons to show on an overhead projector. Visual aids such as drawings, photographs, or objects to pass round (if the group is small) can greatly enhance a presentation. The use of images in this context (a presentation at LEVEL 3) satisfies the requirements of USE IMAGES at LEVEL 3.

Guidance

You do not have to be a skilled artist to draw a sketch. Even matchstick people can make a point. The purpose of using images is to support what is said or written (PC1); by providing images that are appropriate (PC2); and by using the images at appropriate times/places to illustrate clearly the points being made (PC3).

Don't talk down to people

FRANCIS HOUSE

The Ethos of Francis House – fun with care

There is a tendency to run over time when presenting, so Jane may place a watch on the table to check her timing.

Even an experienced speaker may be nervous when talking to a group of strangers, so Jane may take a deep breath, smile warmly and say, with feeling, 'Welcome to Francis House. Thank you for volunteering.'

Guidance

Decide before a presentation whether you will answer questions during or after you have spoken, so that you can make your preference clear to the audience.

 **PRACTICE**

MAKE notes for a presentation, preferably one that you will have to give, either as part of your GNVQ or elsewhere.

- What *could* you talk about – make a list.

- What *should* you talk about (remember who you are talking to; what you are talking about; the attention span of your listeners, etc.).

- Gather or make a few simple images as visual aids to help you illustrate the points you wish to make.

- Decide whether you prefer to answer questions during or after the presentation.

Make the presentation. Review your performance. Did you:

- Keep to the subject and purpose? (PC1).

- Speak in a way suited to your listeners and the formality of the situation? (PC2).

- Use images at appropriate times to clearly illustrate points made? (USE IMAGES: **all** PCS).

- Listen attentively to the questions and contributions of others? (PC3).

- Take forward the discussion by asking questions, summarising or otherwise responding to others' contributions? (PC4).

- Explicitly encourage people to contribute and to ask questions? (LEVEL 3: PC5).

 **HELP**
If you need more help in speaking to groups of people, turn to page 95.

 **EVIDENCE**
Assignment 3 (page 77) provides an opportunity to gather evidence of achievement in speaking to a group of people.

The information sheet for staff

It is important that guests are given a warm welcome to Francis House, and that their immediate needs are met. To remind staff of the procedures, Jane Vaughan produces a handout that they may consult.

Here is Jane's handout on admissions routines:

Guidance

A handout is useful if the information it contains needs to be consulted from time to time and is not readily available elsewhere, for example on a notice board.

When making presentations it is sometimes useful to give handouts rather than having the audience make notes, which may hinder their listening.

 FRANCIS HOUSE

Welcoming and Admitting Guests
1)   Welcome the guest to the building, introduce
     yourself and show them to their room.
2)   Assist as necessary with luggage and equipment.
     Some guests may need help out of vehicles.

Guidance

The handout is written in clearly defined and numbered paragraphs to help the reader follow it step by step. In this way it acts as a checklist for the staff. It satisfies the Performance Criteria for PRODUCE WRITTEN MATERIAL at LEVEL 2: it is about routine matters at Francis House (and is written for staff who will be familiar with procedures).

```
3)  Familiarise them with their own bathroom and give
    them time to use it if they wish.
4)  Make them feel at home by offering them
    tea/coffee, which if they wish may be served in
    their room. (They may need help to drink it. ASK!)
5)  Don't rush them. They may be tired after a long
    journey and may like a little time to themselves
    before the admissions formalities. If you are
    going to leave them, always ensure that they know
    how to contact you through the call system.
6)  Draw their attention to the information sheet with
    details of meal times, outings, etc.
7)  When appropriate, invite the guest to join other
    guests and staff in the lounge. Some may find this
    difficult to do on their own, particularly on a
    first visit.
```

▶ **PRACTICE**   USE any opportunity that presents itself to write a handout or information sheet. Make sure that it satisfies the Performance Criteria for PRODUCE WRITTEN MATERIAL.

 HELP
If you need help to produce written material, turn to page 97.

 **EVIDENCE**
Assignment 12 (page 78) provides an opportunity to produce evidence of achievement in writing a handout.

The questionnaire

Guidance

Questionnaire design requires a lot of thought. Questions should be short and straightforward to avoid misinterpretation. At the same time, many of them need to be open, allowing the respondents to express their views accurately, rather than baldly answering yes or no.

The Centre Manager of Francis House wishes to give each volunteer a simple questionnaire so that she can find out how much they have enjoyed their stay, and in what ways they may have benefited.

The questionnaire can also act as a guide for those who wish to be assessed for GNVQs, or for reports that the Centre Manager may have to write to school and college tutors about the work of learner-volunteers.

Jane Vaughan considers the questions she is going to ask. For instance, one question could be:

Did you enjoy your time here?   Yes/No

The suggested response of Yes/No does not give the respondent an opportunity to express in-between feelings (e.g. they had quite a good time).

A more open form of the question would be:

What did you enjoy most about your stay here? Is there anything you didn't enjoy?

Some questions do need to be posed in a more closed way, calling for Yes/No responses. For example,

Would you volunteer again?   Yes/No

Sub-dividing questions

In order to obtain accurate and useful information, it is sometimes necessary to divide questions into more detailed sub-questions. For example, the open question

How have you found the staff?

would be more useful if it was sub-divided and posed in a closed form:

How helpful have you found the permanent staff?
Very helpful/helpful/not very helpful/unhelpful

How effective do you think teamwork has been?
Very effective/effective/quite effective/ineffective

Finally, it is a good idea in most questionnaires to leave space for people to expand their answers if they wish (e.g. by asking 'Any Other Comments?').

Bearing in mind these principles of questionnaire design, Jane came up with this questionnaire:

Volunteer Questionnaire
I would be grateful if you can spare a few minutes to answer these questions about your stay at Francis House. The information may help the staff to improve our services to guests and volunteers. What you write will remain confidential unless your employer/school/college has agreed with you that a report will be provided, in which case the report may be based partly on your responses.

NAME

Was the placement part of a course (e.g. GNVQ)
Yes/No

How keen were you to work with disabled people?
Very keen/keen/quite keen/not keen

How helpful did you find the permanent staff?
Very helpful/helpful/quite helpful/unhelpful

Do you have any suggestions to improve their helpfulness?

How would you rate the effectiveness of teamwork?
Very effective/effective/quite effective/ineffective

How did you find the quality of the food?
Excellent/good/quite good/awful

In general, how well did you get on with guests?
Very well/well/quite well/badly

Do you think you have learned anything new during your stay? If so, what?

In general, how much do you think you have benefited from your stay?
Benefited greatly/benefited/benefited a little/not benefited at all

Would you volunteer again?
Yes/No

Any other comments?

Thank you for completing the questionnaire

PRACTICE

THERE may be opportunities during your GNVQ course to design a questionnaire and, in doing so, to provide evidence for PRODUCE WRITTEN MATERIAL. The level that it satisfies will depend on how complex the topic is (and who it is written for). A questionnaire on a complex topic may be at LEVEL 3.

Alternatively, choose any topic you think may be interesting to investigate among your fellow learners (e.g. sports activities; tastes in music; career intentions; food likes and dislikes). Design a short questionnaire, taking time to choose its wording with care.

After the questionnaires have been answered and you have gathered the information from them, you may make a short presentation or write a short report on your findings, perhaps illustrated with appropriate images.

HELP
If you need help in designing a questionnaire, turn to page 103.

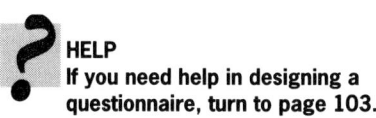 **EVIDENCE**
Assignment 13 (page 78) provides an opportunity to produce evidence of achievement in producing a report.

Letter thanking volunteers

Jane Vaughan writes personally to volunteers after their stay to thank them for their work. She likes to give the letters an individual touch, even though the basic structure of the letter is the same for all volunteers.

The basic structure of the letter is this:

Guidance

Business or work-based letters are not always neutral in tone. Very often the writer will express something of his or her own personality, and will write to the person addressed not just as a customer or colleague, but in a more personal way. Do remember, however, that it is usually obvious if you are being insincere in your writing.

> Thank you for spending time as a volunteer at Francis House. We could not exist without the hard work and generous spirit of people like you.
>
> I hope that in turn you have benefited from your work with us.
>
> Best wishes for the future and thank you once again.
>
> Yours sincerely,
>
>
>
> Jane Vaughan
> The Centre Manager, Francis House.

Jane adds to this basic structure by, for example:

- thanking individuals for any special service they provided, e.g. 'Thank you especially for helping to organise the trip to the Fair';
- thanking individuals for their work with particular guests, e.g. 'Thank you for spending so much time with _____, staying up late with him when he couldn't sleep and still being cheerful in the morning';
- wishing individuals success in their career plans or study, e.g. 'I hope that you gain your GNVQ without problem and that you are successful in finding work in a leisure centre'.

The letter is word processed by Jane's secretary, but Jane prefers to handwrite the greeting herself, e.g. '*Dear Sam*', and to sign her own name.

In her letters, Jane tries not to add insincere praise. Even when a volunteer has not particularly enjoyed working at the Centre, she endeavours to thank them for what they have done, and to give a positive tone to the letter.

 PRACTICE

THERE may be occasions when you need to write a work-related letter that, at the same time, has a personal touch. For example, you may write a letter of thanks to people who took you on work placement; or to staff who helped make your holiday enjoyable. Write the letter and remember to be warm and sincere.

 **HELP**
If you need help with letter writing, turn to page 98.

 **EVIDENCE**
Assignment 11 (page 78) provides an opportunity to produce evidence of achievement in writing a letter.

2   The Dance

The Entertainments Officer at Francis House, David Stubbs, wishes to organise a dance to raise funds in a way that will be enjoyed by volunteers and guests.

The skills as a communicator he will need to employ include:

▶ talking to the Centre Manager to obtain permission
▶ telephoning and/or writing to hire a hall, book a band and/or disco, and arrange a bar licence
▶ contacting local volunteers to request their help with catering, running the bar and selling tickets
▶ designing an advertising poster
▶ reading and responding to letters and memos

Preparing for a meeting with the Centre Manager

Guidance

If a meeting is important, and the people involved are busy, it is wise to do some preparation in advance so that the meeting can be focused and reach its objectives quickly. When preparing for a meeting, people often jot down ideas as a means of thinking through an issue. The notes can then be re-drafted into a neater, more readable format to take to the meeting, perhaps on an index card.

David Stubbs might try to anticipate Jane Vaughan's questions about the proposed dance and to make notes towards answering them:

> Meeting re Dance
>
> Purpose — raise funds
> have a good time
> guests may attend
>
> Profit? — V'teers help sell tickets
> Light supper (fish & chips?)
> Provide a bar – staffed
> by v'teers (I'll handle
> licence)

Jottings – first draft

> Question: Will the dance make money?
> Answer: Yes. Enlist the help of local
> volunteers; include food (provided
> by volunteers) in price; bar profit;
> raffle.
> Q: Will guests be able to participate?
> A: Yes. Those who wish may attend
> with their volunteer helpers, at
> no charge.
> Q: Are there legal and insurance
> problems, especially with a
> licensed bar?
> A: Yes. I will handle all health
> and safety and other
> organisational issues, helped by
> local volunteers.

Final notes for the meeting

 PRACTICE

JUST as the Entertainments Officer made notes, make preliminary notes of the main points to be discussed at a meeting you will attend (e.g. with a tutor, an employer, an experienced employee in your GNVQ area). Then re-draft the notes into a clearer and more logical form for the meeting. Write the final draft on a card or small sheet of paper that you can use during the meeting to jog your memory.

 **HELP**
If you need more help to make notes, turn to page 95.

 **EVIDENCE**
Assignment 6 (page 78) provides an opportunity to produce evidence of achievement in making notes for a meeting.

The meeting itself

The notes you prepare should help you to speak clearly and to the point (DISCUSSION: PC1).

The tone and manner in which David Stubbs speaks to the Centre Manager in an arranged meeting is different to the way he would speak to her over coffee; or the way he would chat to a friend (DISCUSSION: PC2) . He may:

- be more careful in his choice of words
- pronounce his words more clearly
- take more conscious turns to speak and to listen
- use appropriate body language (e.g. the way he sits, maintains eye contact and gives verbal cues, for instance, saying 'Mhm, yes...I agree', to show that he is talking seriously and listening carefully

He would also expect Jane Vaughan's behaviour to be appropriate (e.g. welcoming, listening attentively, clarifying issues, thanking him for his initiative – DISCUSSION PCs 3 and 4).

To avoid confusion later, he may check his understanding of anything Jane Vaughan says that he thinks is unclear (DISCUSSION: PC3) by using phrases such as: 'Do you mean...'; 'I don't quite follow...'; 'Let me check that I've understood you...'.

At the end of the meeting he may thank Jane for her time.

Soon after the meeting he, or Jane, might write a brief note to record what they had agreed.

 PRACTICE

ATTEND the meeting for which you have already prepared. In addition, prepare further by making notes of *how* you will behave, following the worked example above.

After the meeting review how you think it went. Are you happy about your performance, or do you think you need to develop your skills?

At LEVEL 3 it is important to practise talking about *complex matters* (to people who may be *unfamiliar with the subject matter*). Try to estimate how much people will know already; choose your words with care, avoiding difficult or technical terms, or explaining them if you do use them.

 HELP
If you need more help in talking and listening, turn to page 87.

 **EVIDENCE**
Assignment 2 (page 77) provides an opportunity to perform this skill and to produce evidence of achievement in attending a meeting.

Writing a memo to record what has been agreed

To ensure that what was agreed at the meeting is clear so that problems later can be minimised, Jane Vaughan sends David Stubbs a memo. In particular, she was concerned that the dance should not lose money and that, as Entertainments Officer, he should keep personal control of this aspect. The language is therefore brief and to the point, without being threatening.

Guidance

This is a typical memo ('memo' is short for 'memorandum', a note to help the memory). The layout is in a standard format which, in many organisations, is pre-printed. All the writer has to do is fill in the names and date and write the information or request as briefly as possible. It is not necessary to sign a memo.

FRANCIS HOUSE

MEMO

TO: David Stubbs, Entertainments Officer
FROM: Jane Vaughan, Centre Manager
DATE: 2 February
SUBJECT: The dance

Thank you for meeting to discuss the dance. Please go ahead and book a hall and organise a meeting for local volunteers. As agreed, you will take full responsibility for the financial planning and accounting for the event and will not delegate this. Please keep me informed of developments, and good luck with the dance.

 PRACTICE

USE any opportunity that presents itself to write a memo or minutes from a meeting. Try to record what has been agreed briefly and plainly so that there is no ambiguity or doubt.

 HELP
If you need help in writing memos, turn to page 98.

 **EVIDENCE**
Assignment 9 (page 78) provides an opportunity to produce evidence of achievement in writing a memo.

Using the telephone

Guidance

When using the telephone we do not have the usual range of clues to know how the other person is reacting to what we say. We can't see their eyes, their facial expressions, or their body posture. In consequence, we sometimes feel uncertain and even nervous. To help overcome this *prepare* to use the telephone by making notes; try to relax and talk in a normal voice, at a normal pace.

When to use the telephone

David Stubbs wishes to hire a hall for the dance. He needs information about a number of halls: size, capacity, licensing for music and dancing, costs, dates available, etc. He has a number of options:

He could write to a number of halls – in which case he would need to wait for replies and then he may need to write again to clarify points.

He could visit a number of halls – but this would be time-consuming, and they may be shut, or the person he needs to talk to may not be there.

The most efficient way to contact the halls is to use the telephone. David's first task is to make some notes to clarify what he wishes to find out:

Size of hall
Cost
Licensing arrangements
Speakers & mikes
Dates available

Unless he holds the names and numbers of halls on file, the next step is to use *Yellow Pages* or another local telephone guide. Under the word 'Halls' he finds a list of possible venues for the dance from which to select.

He then telephones a number of halls to obtain the information he needs, making a note of their replies beside their names and telephone numbers.

Using images to record information: a table

In order to record information clearly and simply, David draws up a simple table, like this:

Hall name	Tel.	Capacity	Licence?	Kitchen	Cost	Dates

He may need to call back to talk to someone who has the information he needs, or to check further details. Eventually he will be ready to make a decision and to send a letter to confirm a booking.

 PRACTICE

Guidance

Most directories have sections at the front and/or back that explain how to use the directory. Most are arranged in alphabetical order. The best way to get to know a directory is to **use** it.

For some searches in *Yellow Pages* (e.g. 'CD-ROM') it may be necessary to consult the *Classification Index* at the back for alternative sections (e.g. **Computers**: peripherals or **Audio Dealers**: TV, video & radio shops). In case of real difficulty it is possible to phone *Talking Pages*, but there is a charge for this service.

Making a telephone call: choose a topic about which you need information. It may be connected with your GNVQ (e.g. the cost of hiring halls for wedding receptions; the availability of local work placements) or with your personal life (e.g. the costs and times of alternative forms of travel to a particular destination; the cost of a particular CD-ROM system).

Write notes about the information you need and prepare a table to record the information you obtain.

Reading: consult *Yellow Pages* or another local directory and search for suitable numbers. (Telephone directories are used routinely in all organisations, and follow a pre-set format, therefore their use is at LEVEL 1.)

Make notes of important points discussed during the call.

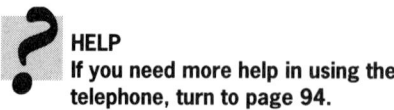 **HELP**
If you need more help in using the telephone, turn to page 94.

 **EVIDENCE**
Assignment 4 (page 77) provides an opportunity to produce evidence of achievement in using the telephone.

Reading: level 3: clarifying meaning

During his telephone conversations, David Stubbs asks a number of hall managers to send further details of halls that sounded suitable. Here is one letter he received:

```
                                  New Hall,
                                  Excise Road,
                                  Seaton.
                                  14 February, 199_

Dear Sir,
Thank you for your telephone enquiry about hiring the
hall. It can take about 220 people, although this
depends on what they are doing — sitting, dancing and
so on. Say 180? The toilets are OK for the number.
Here is a plan:
```

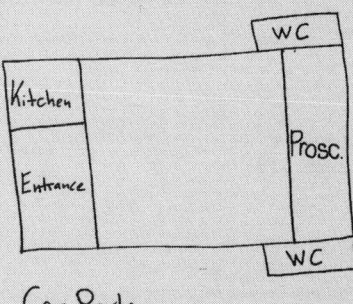

```
As you can see, there is a car park. The decibels need
to be controlled because of the neighbours. Disabled
access, including wheelchair, no problem. Let me know
if you want it.


Yours sincerely,


James Macpherson
Hall Manager
```

David read the letter and was puzzled by a number of points: how many people **can** the hall accommodate for dancing? What is meant by the toilets being 'OK'? How many vehicles can be parked? Does the reference to decibels and neighbours refer to the cars, or to the music, or both? What does the final 'it' refer to – the hall or wheelchair access?

He was also uncertain about the terms 'prosc.' (on the plan) and 'decibel'.

The subject of the letter is straightforward, but its lack of clarity, and the need for the Entertainments Officer to take responsibility for clarifying points, makes this LEVEL 3.

David consulted a dictionary to check the meanings of 'prosc.' which turned out to be short for 'proscenium' (a stage with an enclosing arch), and 'decibel' (a measure of the intensity of sound). The definition of 'decibel' did not help him much, because it gave no indication of how many decibels are regarded as intense sound. So he consulted a single-volume encyclopedia and read that a whisper is about 20 dB ('dB' is an

Guidance

In order to identify and clarify the meaning of words, it is sometimes necessary to consult a simple encyclopedia, because a standard dictionary may not provide sufficient information.

abbreviation for 'decibels') and a jet taking off nearby is about 140dB (which is on the threshold of pain). He was still uncertain – how many decibels would a band produce? And what level of sound would be tolerated by the neighbours?

At this stage David may have given up considering this hall, but, because it was available on the night required, was conveniently located, and was affordable he telephoned the Hall Manager in order to clarify what he had written.

 PRACTICE

WHEN you read letters or other documents that are.unclear in their meaning, use appropriate sources of reference to clarify your understanding (READING: PC3). These may include dictionaries, encyclopedias, and consulting other people. For evidence purposes, remember to keep a record of what you clarified, and by what means.

 HELP
If you need help in using sources to clarify meaning, turn to page 125.

 **EVIDENCE**
Assignment 21 (page 80) provides an opportunity to produce evidence of achievement in using sources of reference.

The letter of confirmation

Guidance

• Business letters should be as brief as possible, while including all relevant information (PC1).
• The letter should be typed or written legibly and the meaning should be clear (PC2).
• Standard conventions of spelling, punctuation and grammar should be followed (PC3).
• The letter should be organised to maximise the reader's understanding – in this case the purpose of the letter and key information are stated in the first paragraph. Further paragraphs go into more detail. The letter ends politely (PC5).

Once David Stubbs has agreed by telephone to book a hall, he decides to write a brief letter of confirmation so that both he, and the hall staff, will have a record of the agreement.

In this case the letter is at LEVEL 2, because the Hall Manager, for whom the letter is written, is familiar with the subject; and the subject matter is routine.

Here is David's letter:

```
                                        FRANCIS HOUSE
                                        The Promenade
                                        Seaton
                                        1S HL1

                                        16 February 199

James Macpherson
Hall Manager
New Hall
Excise Road
Seaton

Dear Mr Macpherson,

Hall Booking

Following our recent telephone conversation, I am writing to
confirm a booking of the hall on 23 June between 6.00 p.m. and
1.00 a.m. at the agreed price of £100.00.
     As you know, we will hold a dance and would therefore like
tables and chairs to be arranged round the edge of the hall,
with the central area free for dancing.
     The band will bring and set up their own sound system but will
need power. We will set up a bar, using volunteer helpers, who
will need washing-up facilities. As agreed, we will bring our
own glasses and washing materials and will clean the bar area
and kitchen after use.
```

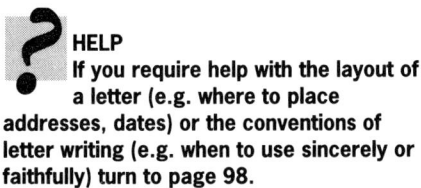

Thank you for your cooperation in helping us to organise the event.

Yours sincerely,

David Stubbs
Entertainments Officer

? HELP
If you require help with the layout of a letter (e.g. where to place addresses, dates) or the conventions of letter writing (e.g. when to use sincerely or faithfully) turn to page 98.

EVIDENCE
Assignment 11 (page 78) provides an opportunity to produce evidence of achievement in writing a letter.

Using images to illustrate a point: a sketch

David draws a simple sketch to show the Hall Manager how he wishes the hall to be laid out, and attaches it to the letter:

Guidance

The sketch satisfies the Performance Criteria for ELEMENT 2.3: USE IMAGES. It illustrates clearly where David Stubbs wishes the table placed (PC1); although it is roughly drawn, it suits its purpose and will be understood by the Hall Manager (PC2); it is appropriate to attach it to the letter so that it may be detached and given to the staff who will place the tables (PC3).

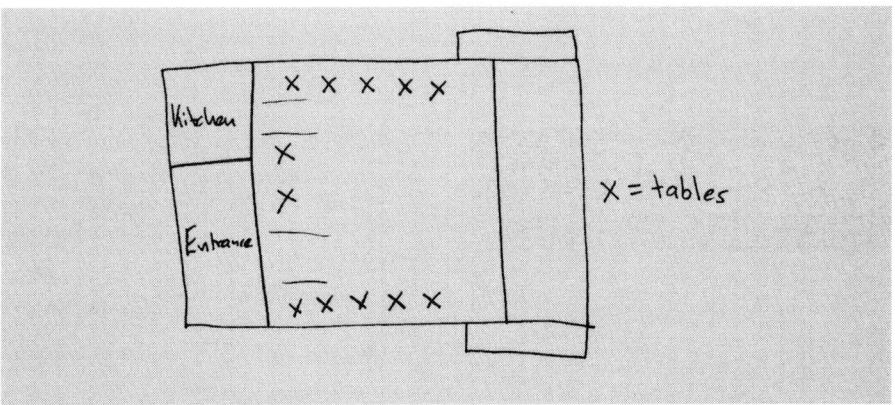

▶ PRACTICE

WRITING brief, informative letters takes practice. Be patient. Draft your letters and show them to a friend for comment – how easily can they be read? Are they clear?

Use any real opportunity to write letters (e.g. a letter to your Bank Manager requesting an overdraft; a letter to an employer asking if there is any part-time work available). Keep all letters and replies to use as evidence of achievement.

When you write or speak to people, consider whether at any point it would be helpful to use an image, such as a simple sketch.

? HELP
If you need help to use images, turn to page 117.

EVIDENCE
Assignment 18 (page 79) provides an opportunity to produce evidence of achievement in drawing a sketch.

The letter to local volunteers

The Francis House Centre Manager, Jane Vaughan, has asked David Stubbs to let her see a draft of a letter that he has written to be circulated to local volunteers, asking them to help organise and run the dance. She is concerned that the tone of the letter should be appropriate because she knows that people are busy and that many already give generously of their time. She does not want the letter to sound too pressing.

Here is the draft of David's letter:

> Dear Friend,
>
> I am writing to let you know that we intend to organise a dance to raise funds for Francis House and, at the same time, have a good time. I am sure you have now guessed what this letter is about — can you spare a little time to help?
>
> All the staff at Francis House are already aware of the time and energy that so many people give freely to help make guests' stay here a happy one. We also realise how busy you are. However, if you can spare some time to sell tickets or to help out on the night (bar, buffet, etc.) then please let me know.
>
> Best wishes,
>
> etc.

If you were the Centre Manager would you suggest any amendments to this letter before it is sent to volunteers?

Jane Vaughan made these suggestions:

> Dear (Friend,)   *use name - mailmerge*
>
> I am writing to let you know that we ~~intend to organise~~ *are organising* a dance, to raise funds for Francis House and, at the same time, have a good *(enjoy ourselves)* time. I am sure you have now guessed what this letter is about — *avoids repetition of word 'time'* can you spare a little time to help?
>
> ~~All~~ The staff at Francis House are already aware of the time and energy that so many people give freely to help make guests' stay here a happy one. We also realise how busy you are. However, *be clearer about help needed* if you can spare some time to sell tickets or to help out on the night (bar, buffet, etc.) then please let me know.
>
> Best wishes,
>
> etc.

I like the letter and think the tone is about right. We have a list of volunteers' names on computer, so you can use the mailmerge facility to make the letters more personal.

I think a fuller explanation of 'help' is needed — perhaps something like 'serving behind the bar, providing some food for a buffet, helping to clean the hall after the dance'.

Rather than contacting you, I think it would be preferable to hold an informal meeting for volunteers, with tea and biscuits.

<table>
<tr><td>

Guidance

Feelings can hinder understanding. Whether reading or listening, it is easy for our feelings (pride, anger, resentment, etc.) to get in the way of understanding. The Entertainments Officer could have thought, 'How dare she criticise my letter!', and as a result may have ignored her suggestions.

</td></tr>
</table>

Jane's reading and response is at LEVEL 3, because she is making judgements about the suitability of David's letter and needs to deal with it (and the volunteers) sensitively. David read the suggestions and did not feel offended by them because he had drafted the letter quite quickly and knew that Jane's ideas were meant to be constructive. Another person can often see straight away what a writer may miss entirely.

David read Jane's note and extracted the following four main points (READING: PC4):

- the letter should be personalised
- its use of language should be improved
- the help needed should be stated clearly
- a meeting should be held

He had no need to check the meaning of any part of the letter.

 PRACTICE

READ material that is sent to you and try to be aware of how your feelings can sometimes interfere with your comprehension. In fact, understanding is often a combination of thought and feeling but, if feelings overwhelm thought, much can be missed.

 HELP
If you need help in extracting information from your reading, turn to page 125.

 **EVIDENCE**
Assignment 22 (page 80) provides an opportunity to produce evidence of achievement in reading newspaper reports.

Re-drafting

David Stubbs re-wrote the letter, incorporating Jane's ideas. Here is the re-draft, in which David also included new ideas:

```
                              FRANCIS HOUSE
                              The Promenade
                              Seaton
                              1S HL1


                              [Date]

   Dear [Name of person],
   I am writing to seek your help. We are organising a
dance to raise funds for Francis House and, at the
same time, to enjoy ourselves. Can you spare a little
time to help?
   The staff at Francis House are aware of the time and
energy that so many people give freely to help make
guests' stay a happy one. We also realise how busy
people are. However, if you can spare some time it
would be much appreciated. We need volunteers to, for
example:
   · sell tickets
   · make some food for a buffet
   · serve behind the bar
```

```
     If you think you can help in any way, please come
along for a cup of tea and an informal meeting on
Thursday March 23rd at 6.30 p.m.
  Best wishes,
```

David Stubbs
Entertainments Officer

▶ PRACTICE

RE-READ one or two letters that you have already written and re-draft them to improve:

- what you have written: can anything unnecessary be taken out? Can anything be added to improve the letter's accuracy or clarity? (PC1)

- the legibility of the handwriting, or spacing, typeface and typesize (PC2)

- the spelling, punctuation and grammar (PC3)

- the organisation of the letter, and your choice of words, in order to make it easier for the reader to understand (PC5)

Whether the letter is at LEVEL 2 or 3 will depend on how complex (or sensitive) the subject is (and on how familiar the audience is to you and with the subject matter).

HELP
If you need help with any aspect of letter writing, turn to page 98.

EVIDENCE

Assignment 10 (page 78) provides an opportunity to produce evidence of achievement in re-drafting material.

The informal meeting for volunteers

Prior to the meeting David Stubbs drew up a list of the tasks he would like volunteers to take responsibility for. He wrote them on a flipchart. Listing the tasks on a flipchart will allow people to see them clearly and to put their names against specific tasks. The list is shown on the next page:

> Dance
>
> VOLUNTEERS NEEDED:
>
> BAR: one energetic person is needed to manage these tasks:
>
> • purchase drinks and hire glasses
> • set up the bar
> • arrange a rota of bar staff
> • arrange for cleaning of tables and washing of glasses
> • arrange for clearing away
> • arrange for returns of unused drinks and hired glasses and draw up the bar account, including costs of breakages
>
> Ten people are needed for a Bar staff rota
>
> FOOD: one brave person is needed to manage these tasks:
> Draw up a list of food required
> Liaise with volunteers who will prepare food
> Purchase paper plates, napkins, etc.
> Arrange for serving of food and clearing of tables
> Arrange for cleaning of kitchen
>
> Lots of people to prepare and bring food
> Six people to serve food and clear up
>
> PROMOTION: Ten people needed to put posters in shops, etc.
>
> Lots of people to sell tickets

Guidance

If a meeting is to reach its objectives quickly then a certain amount of organising and thinking through of issues needs to be done in advance. This is what the Entertainments Officer has done in this example.

Using images to illustrate points: a chart

In order to help the volunteers to see at a glance what help is needed, David Stubbs draws a simple chart of the tasks, like this:

Guidance

The chart is at LEVEL 3, because it supports a LEVEL 3 meeting at which David has to deal tactfully with people to encourage volunteers. It is simple but effective, using few words and images for maximum impact.

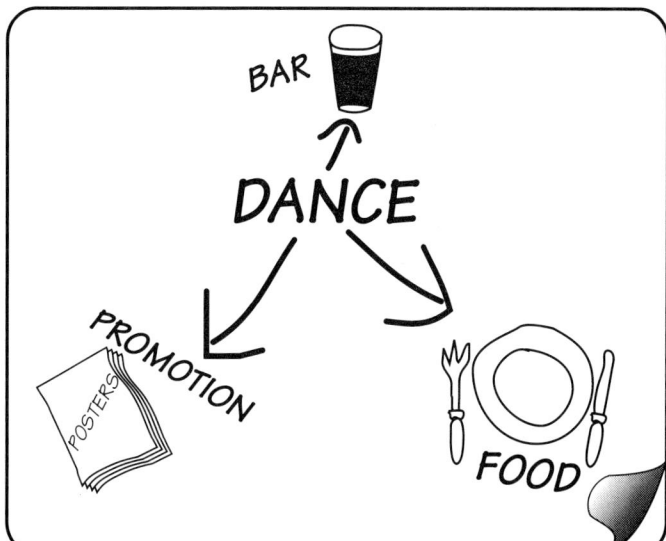

HELP
If you need help to use images, turn to page 117.

 **E V I D E N C E**
Assignment 8 (page 78) provides an opportunity to produce evidence of achievement in producing a chart.

Guidance

At any meeting when people are being asked to do things, tact is needed (a sense of the appropriate thing to say), especially when people are volunteers. Remember, however, that tact does not mean dishonesty.

The meeting is at LEVEL 3 because the subject is complex (and the audience are not familiar with it).

At the meeting

David waited with bated breath to see if any volunteers turned up for the meeting. Quite a few did. He made them welcome, and gave them tea and biscuits to make them feel relaxed and valued. Because he did not know everyone's name, he passed round a sheet of paper to record who was present.

David explained the purpose of the meeting (to find volunteers to help organise a dance) and exactly what help was required by showing them the list he had drawn up and the chart.

There then followed a discussion about what exactly would be involved, and in some cases whether tasks could be shared between a number of people. Then came decision time, when people were asked to express an interest in taking on one of the main management roles – for the bar and the food. There was silence. People who did not wish to volunteer avoided David's eye. Then there was a little embarrassed laughter. Eventually, two brave souls volunteered and the atmosphere became more relaxed again. Once some people had volunteered to take on a lot of responsibility, there was a rush of other people to help them and to sell tickets. By the end of the meeting David was very pleased.

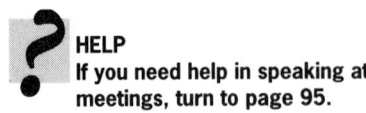 **P R A C T I C E**

PREPARE for a meeting by drawing up a list of the points that you think should be covered. Use images if appropriate to make these points clear. The meeting does not necessarily have to be one arranged by you. Your points could refer only to those things that you personally think important.

Attend the meeting and try *tactfully* to raise and deal with the points on your list. Remember to follow the Performance Criteria for TAKE PART IN DISCUSSIONS:

• Make contributions which are relevant to the subject and purpose (PC1).

• Make contributions in a way that is suited to the audience and situation (PC2).

• Listen attentively and confirm that you have understood the contributions of others (PC3).

• Make contributions which take forward the discussion (PC4).

• At LEVEL 3, create opportunities for others to contribute (PC5).

 **HELP**
If you need help in speaking at meetings, turn to page 95.

 **E V I D E N C E**
Assignment 6 (page 78) provides an opportunity to produce evidence of achievement in preparing for a meeting.

The minutes of the meeting

In order that there is no doubt about who had agreed to do what, and in order to keep the Centre Manager informed, David wrote minutes of the meeting to circulate to all who would help with the dance.

> **FRANCIS HOUSE**
> Minutes of the meeting held on 23 March to discuss the organisation of a dance.
>
> **Present:** David Stubbs (Chair), Hasan Alman, Emma Davison, Maria Dodds, Michelle Firth, Paul Gooding, Kate Huckle, Aidan Jones, Tanya Kumari, Helen O'Donnell, Simon Offord, Alison Mackenzie, Mike Monroe, Carl Russell, Anthony Santos, Raymond Soma, Mary Wong
> **Apologies** (phoned and wanted to help, but couldn't make meeting): Mark Bentley, Kirsten Brenner, Liam Connolly, Steven Grant, Linda Hayes, Karen Humphries, Sara Ingham, Deepak Voraj
>
> 1) The Entertainments Officer (David Stubbs) agreed to hire a hall and a band. He will also design and print a public notice, purchase tickets and liaise with ticket sellers. He also agreed that he will handle all financial matters: ticket monies should be returned to him; bills for drinks etc. should be sent to him for payment.
> 2) Alison Mackenzie agreed to manage the bar. She will make arrangements to order drinks, hire glasses and draw up a rota of staff to set up, run and clear away the bar.
> 3) Paul Gooding agreed to manage the food. He will liaise with other volunteers to ensure a suitable variety of food; and to staff the evening. It was agreed that plastic plates and cutlery will be used.
> 4) A number of people volunteered to put up notices and sell tickets. When these are available, they will be distributed by David Stubbs.
> 5) A Dance Planning Committee was set up, of four people (David Stubbs, Alison Mackenzie, Paul Gooding and Emma Davison, a local solicitor, who has kindly agreed to be responsible for licensing and meeting Health & Safety requirements). The Committee will meet on 17 April at Francis House.
> 6) The Entertainments Officer would like to thank everyone who came along. Thank you for your help.

Guidance

The purpose of minutes is to record briefly what has been discussed and agreed at a meeting. In some cases, for example with official company meetings, the minutes may act as a record of what was agreed, which may be used as evidence in a court of law. It is important, therefore, that minutes are accurate and so they are usually presented to the next meeting for comment and approval as an accurate record.

▶ **PRACTICE**

USE any opportunity that presents itself to draw up the minutes of a meeting. Read the minutes of meetings to see how they usually follow a set format, designed to set out the record as plainly as possible.

 HELP
If you need more help in writing minutes of meetings, turn to page 102.

 **EVIDENCE**
Assignment 7 (page 78) provides an opportunity to produce evidence of achievement in writing the minutes of a meeting.

Designing tickets and a poster

Francis House does not have the resources to pay for the services of a professional designer, so David does his best to produce designs that can be duplicated on a photocopier.

Here is David's attempt at designing a ticket:

The poster

David wants a simple poster for volunteers to put up in local shop windows. Here is his attempt:

▶ **PRACTICE**

USE any opportunity that presents itself to use layout to enhance meaning, and to use sketches or other images to illustrate and aid communication.

 HELP
If you need help in using images, turn to page 117.

 **EVIDENCE**
Assignment 16 (page 79) provides an opportunity to produce evidence of achievement in using layout to communicate more effectively.

Providing feedback on the dance

Using images: a pie chart

After the dance David Stubbs decides to show staff and volunteers (particularly local volunteers who contributed time, food, drink, etc.) how much money was raised and where it went. After some thought, he concludes that a pie chart would be the clearest means of expressing the information. It will be relevant and support what he wishes to say about the success of the dance (USE IMAGES: PC1); it will present information clearly to the volunteers (PC2); and he will use it at an appropriate place, in a letter to volunteers thanking them for their help (PC3).

Here is David's chart:

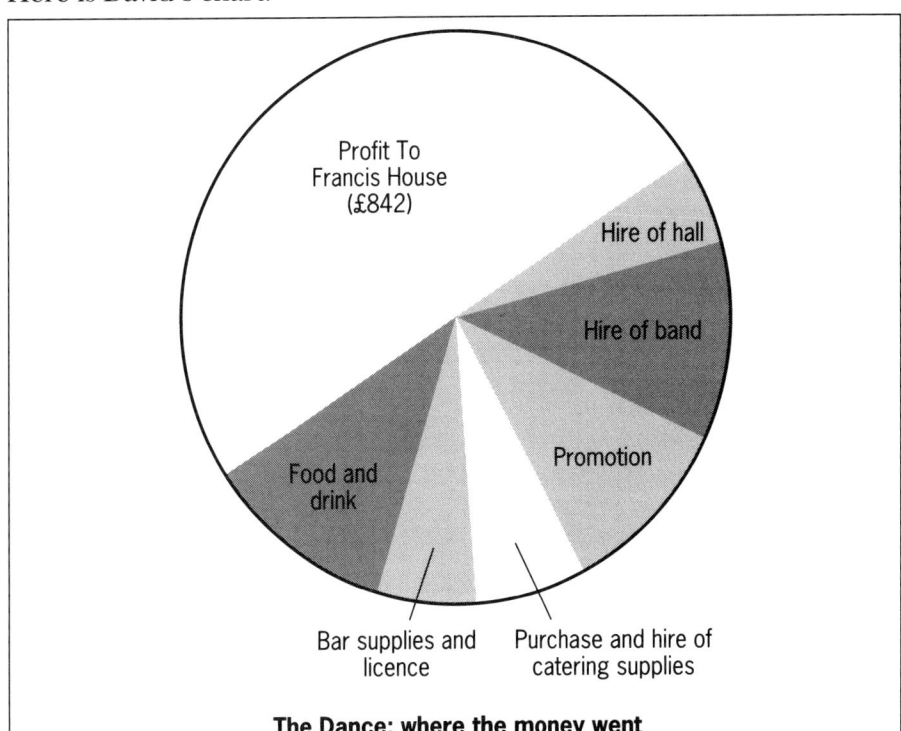

The Dance: where the money went

Guidance

A pie chart is useful when there is one complete total to be shown divided into its differentiated parts. It cannot show change over time (a graph or bar chart would be better for this, with two axes, one of which is used to show time); and it may become confusing if there are too many divisions (in which case it would be better to use a table or bar chart).

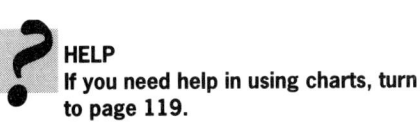

HELP
If you need help in using charts, turn to page 119.

EVIDENCE

Assignment 17 (page 79) provides an opportunity to produce evidence of achievement in presenting statistical information.

Reading complex materials at LEVEL 3

A local volunteer who helped with the dance asked David to give a talk about leisure activities to a local club. As part of his preparation for the talk, David scanned and skimmed a number of books and articles (READING: PC1), extracted information that would be useful for his talk by making notes (PC2) and clarified his understanding when necessary (PC3). Finally, he summarised the information (PC4) for his talk.

One passage he found puzzling was this:

AREAS OF SELF-ACTUALISATION. Respondents were asked to distribute one hundred hours of unexpected free time among five areas in any way they wished. Findings showed the following distribution of average hours allotted to five potential areas of self-actualisation:

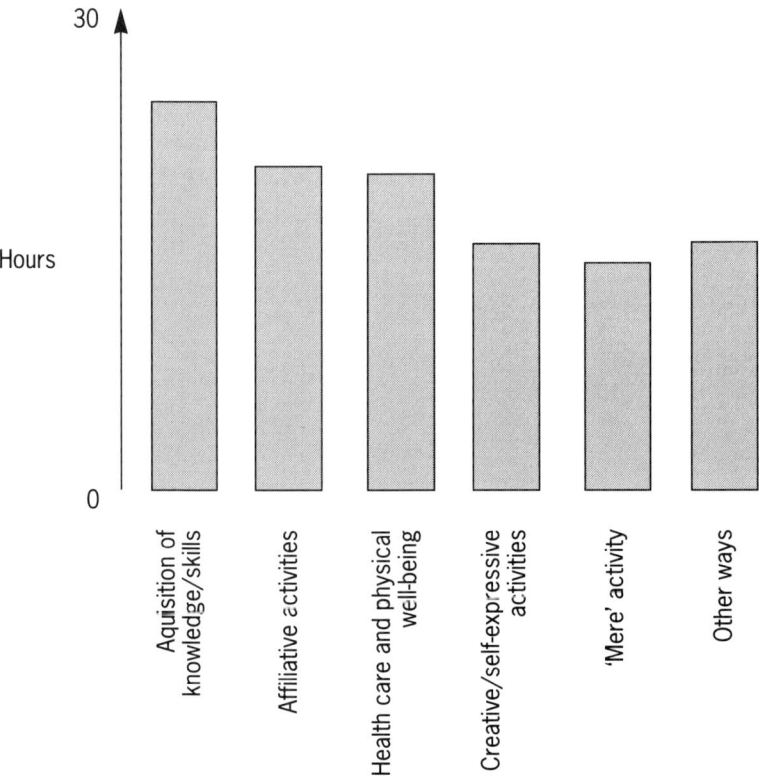

Average hours allotted to five potential areas of self-actualisation

The most striking finding seems to be the fact that no one area predominates as a choice. The fact that there is diversity in the group, as a whole, does not imply that the choices made were not meaningful for the individual. A detailed analysis of two of these alternatives revealed that one's choice of area of self-actualisation indeed relates to one's overall view of the leisure domain and, it is probably safe to assume, way beyond that.

(Adapted from John Neulinger, 1976, *The Psychology of Leisure* Charles Thomas, Springfield, Ill.)

Guidance

It is sometimes necessary to consult a number of sources for clarification of terms before they become clear. It is also necessary to return frequently to the original to see the meaning in context.

David was puzzled about what point the passage was making about people's use of leisure time. First of all, there were a number of words and phrases that he did not altogether understand: 'self-actualisation'; 'affiliative activities'; 'mere activity'; and the whole of the last two sentences.

To clarify understanding (PC3) he first of all consulted the index of the book where he saw that the term 'self-actualisation' had been used earlier. He turned to the page reference given and read, 'self-actualisation…a broadening of the self', and '…self-actualisation. By this term was meant a force basic to the nature of man'. He was still unclear about the meaning of the term, but turned to 'affiliative activities'. In the index he found references to 'Activities' which he followed up to give him the idea that 'affiliative activities' referred to leisure pursuits that involved joining with others in clubs, sports, etc.

Returning to the term 'self-actualisation', he consulted a dictionary but could find no reference to it; and then a single-volume encyclopedia, without success. He then showed the passage to a colleague and asked her if she could explain. She was not entirely sure, but believed the term meant 'the desire to reach one's full human potential'. With this knowledge, David re-read the passage.

He struggled with the last two sentences and concluded that they meant that, regardless of what leisure interests other people may have, each individual is entitled to their own interest; and an individual's choice depends on all sorts of factors about their background and what is available to them.

 PRACTICE

USE any opportunity that arises to read books and articles. Remember that it may be necessary to dip into several books, rather than studying one in depth in order to obtain the information you need. Make use of dictionaries, encyclopedias, and people to help you clarify meaning. Be prepared to be persistent if you wish to understand complex writing fully.

? HELP
If you need help to read effectively, turn to page 123.

 **EVIDENCE**
Assignment 20 (page 80) provides an opportunity to produce evidence of achievement in reading to find out information.

3 Catering for pleasure

Guests' happiness on holiday is partly the result of the quality of the food. Helen Donovan, the Catering Manager at Francis House, works hard to provide tasty meals for the holidaymakers, many of whom have special diets.

Mealtimes are also made enjoyable by meeting people in a friendly, relaxed atmosphere. The volunteer helpers join guests at mealtimes, to give assistance if necessary, but mainly to socialise and get to know people.

Helen sees part of her job as encouraging her team of staff and volunteers to help create a welcoming atmosphere. The communication skills that she needs to use include:

▶ advising and directing staff and volunteers
▶ using the telephone to obtain and exchange information
▶ writing a variety of documents, including menus, memos and diet charts
▶ using images to convey information, for example about health and safety
▶ reading a variety of documents, from diet charts to books

Creating a sense of teamwork

Guidance

People do not like attending meetings if they seem to have little point. Make sure that meetings are necessary and, if possible, enjoyable. Circulate papers in advance. Have an agenda. Provide some refreshments.

Helen needs to have skills that explicitly encourage people to contribute (DISCUSSION LEVEL 3: PC5) so that she builds the team spirit necessary to meet the needs of the guests. Towards the beginning of each week she calls a brief team meeting for all new volunteers and some staff.

The Catering Manager's agenda for a meeting

1) Talking to guests (smile, listen, talk normally)

2) Dealing with difficulties – talk to *appropriate* member of staff (not always me)

3) Questions/anxieties

During the meeting Helen encourages everyone to contribute, even those who may be shy in unfamiliar surroundings. She may do this by:

> giving everyone an opportunity to talk early in the meeting (e.g. by asking everyone to say their name and where they come from);
> asking people by name for their opinions about matters being discussed.

Helen will try to end the meeting on time and on a positive note by thanking everyone for attending and for their contributions.

 PRACTICE

TAKE part in a team meeting (not necessarily as the Chair of the meeting). Do your best to contribute as much as is appropriate and, if you can, to encourage others to contribute as well.

After the meeting review the activity against the Performance Criteria for TAKE PART IN DISCUSSIONS on pages 6 and 10. How well did you do?

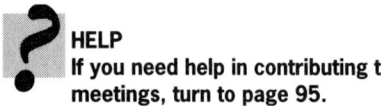 **HELP**
If you need help in contributing to meetings, turn to page 95.

 **EVIDENCE**
Assignment 3 (page 77) provides an opportunity to produce evidence of achievement in speaking to a group of people.

Talking to guests

Volunteers may be unused to talking to strangers, especially to those who are a very different age and who may have physical disabilities. When Helen Donovan helps volunteers who have difficulty in talking to guests she gives the following advice:

> The golden rule is not to patronise or talk down to people, regardless of their age or disability. Be yourself, and expect the other person to be natural with you.
> As you get to know the other person more, you may become genuinely friendly. How do you converse with a friend? There is likely to be a certain amount of good-natured give and take. The underlying feeling is one of mutual support and respect. Within

this supportive framework you may occasionally even make fun of one another.

Listening is just as important as speaking. Sometimes people are uncertain about what they will talk about when all they need do is lend a sympathetic ear and encourage the other person to talk.

Using images: a diagram

In order to help volunteers remember the key points about talking to guests, a member of staff put up a poster in the staff rest room:

Guidance

The poster meets the requirements of USE IMAGES: it illustrates clearly the points the Catering Manager made (PC1); it is suited to its audience (PC2); and it is used in an appropriate place – it may not be suited to display to guests in the dining room (PC3).

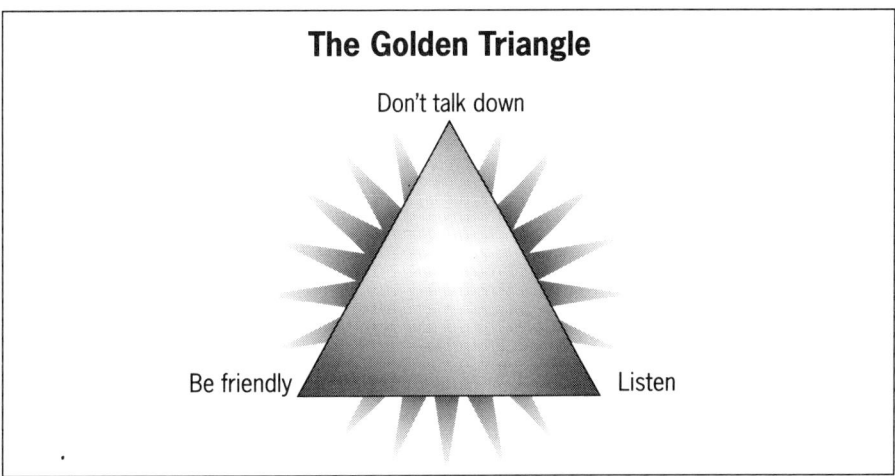

The Golden Triangle

Don't talk down

Be friendly   Listen

 PRACTICE

MAKE notes of how effectively you speak and listen to people in different situations. Pay special attention to conversing with people with whom you do not come into frequent contact; and with people who may not know much about the subject.

Use images to help you make points clearly, especially when presenting ideas and information to people who may know little about the subject.

Make a few tape recordings of yourself talking and listening. You may do this collaboratively with a friend who is also interested in monitoring their speaking and listening.

How happy are you with your skills?

 HELP
If you need more help in speaking and listening turn to page 87.

 **EVIDENCE**
Assignment 1 (page 77) provides an opportunity to produce evidence of achievement in taking part in one-to-one discussions.

Catering for guests' needs

Some guests at Francis House will dislike certain foods, but will not require a special diet; other guests will have a diet that must be strictly followed on medical advice, or for religious reasons. Thus it is necessary to record clearly any special dietary requirements.

Guidance

Notice that, in common with many charts, there are two axes. In this case the vertical axis is used for guests' names, and the horizontal one for dietary needs. If they were placed the other way round the sheet would need to be very wide to include all 26 guests across; or a number of separate sheets would be required. So, choose which variable goes on which axis according to convenience.

Using images: a diet chart

To make it easy to assess guests' needs at a glance, Helen Donovan designs a diet chart on which each guest's requirements can be entered:

Special dietary requirements (please tick or cross as appropriate)

	Sugar	Salt	Fat	Gluten	Halal	Kosher	Other
Name							

 **P R A C T I C E**

DESIGN a simple chart to record information. Consider carefully what should go along the two axes of the chart.

 HELP
If you need help to use charts, turn to page 119.

 E V I D E N C E
Assignment 17 (page 79) provides an opportunity to produce evidence of achievement in presenting information in a chart.

Reading for menu planning

Helen often consults recipe books to give her fresh ideas about menus. She reads the following table and its accompanying text from a guide for caterers:

Creams and yoghurts	% fat	Cheeses	% fat
Clotted cream	55	Cream cheese	45
Double cream	48	Lymeswold	37
Whipping cream	40	Stilton	35
Crème fraîche	30	Cheddar	34
Single cream	18	Vegetarian cheddar	33
Soured cream	18	Gruyère	33
Half cream	12	Parmesan	29
'Total' Greek yoghurt	10	Edam	23
Natural low-fat yoghurt	0.75	Curd cheese	12
		Fromage frais	0.4–8
		Cottage cheese	4
		Ricotta cheese	4
		Quark	0–10

Guidance

Notice that in this table the foods are listed in order of fat content, to make it easier for the reader to extract the information.

The recipes in this book hardly use cream in any form, and where hard fatty cheeses such as Gruyère or Parmesan are selected for their special flavour, yoghurt is used in tandem with low-fat natural yoghurt, in order to limit overall fat content. For the 'Parslied Chicken', a fresh herb stuffing is made with fromage blanc – a combination of cottage cheese, yoghurt and lemon juice. The stuffing is carefully placed under the skin, so that the flavours permeate the chicken during cooking.

Although health faddists were once cruelly caricatured by Alexei Sayle as 'weaving their own yoghurt', today yoghurt has shed its cranky image and emerged as a regular component of the national diet. It contains all the nutrients of skimmed milk and its bacteria can be useful in combating infections; for example, the lactobacilli found in live yoghurt have been shown to clear up digestive disorders

(Rob Silverstone, 1990, *Healthy Eating*, Macmillan)

Guidance

Reading is not always a linear activity, in which you start at the beginning of a document and read to the end, Sometimes you scan a document to find the parts that concern you, and then skim these for information.

Two words gave Helen pause for thought: 'caricature', a word she had often heard but without fully understanding its meaning; and 'lactobacilli', which she had never encountered before. She consulted a dictionary (READ AND RESPOND: use appropriate sources of reference) and read that 'caricature is a grotesque exaggeration of certain traits in an individual'. So in this context, it meant that a liking for yoghurt was pounced upon and exaggerated for comic effect, while other characteristics of the people (which might show them in a different light) were ignored.

Helen could not find 'lactobacilli' in the dictionary. However, she read that 'lacto' refers to milk and already knew that 'bacilli' are micro-organisms.

 PRACTICE

WHEN you need to read documents (books, articles, reports, etc.) try to select an appropriate method of reading – do you need to study each page, and read the whole document; or is it preferable to scan read, slowing down only when you need to skim the parts that are of real interest?
What do you think are the main points made in the above passage?

Helen drew two main points from what she read (READ AND RESPOND: extract the necessary information [PC2] and summarise the information extracted [PC3]):

- It is possible to mix high-fat ingredients with low-fat ingredients to produce a mixture that is flavoursome and healthy.
- Live yoghurt contains micro-organisms that can combat infections and digestive disorders.

 PRACTICE

WHEN you read books, articles and papers, check on the meanings of unfamiliar words and phrases. Try to identify the main points being made – sometimes it helps to summarise these in note form.

 HELP
If you need help in making notes from what you read, turn to page 127.

 **EVIDENCE**
Assignment 24 (page 80) provides an opportunity to produce evidence of achievement in reading and responding to statistical information.

Dealing with complaints

Guidance

Every complaint should be taken seriously. It would be wrong, however, to jump to conclusions such as, 'That volunteer is useless, I knew it all the time'; or 'You're a born complainer. You'll complain that your grave is too wide'.

Guidance

Most complaints can be dealt with by listening and responding sensitively, without need for time-consuming form filling, involvement of other people, or argument.

Occasionally staff have to deal with complaints about, for example, the standards of food, or the cleanliness of rooms.

A member of the staff receives a complaint from a guest that the volunteer assigned to clean his room is slapdash and that the room is a 'pigsty'.

The member of staff may take the following steps:

First of all she should listen attentively to the complaint (DISCUSSION: PC3) and, if necessary, should ask questions to check that she has understood the nature of the complaint (DISCUSSION: PC3).

Then, she should do one of two things: if there is time, accompany the guest to his room to see for herself; or tell the guest that the complaint will be looked into as soon as possible.

If she looks at the room herself, the nature of 'pigsty' will become clearer (e.g. the sink is slightly grubby, and a vacuum cleaner has not been used every day). Having a better idea of what is bothering the guest, the member of staff could say something clear and appropriate (DISCUSSION: PC1), in a tone and manner suited to the person she is speaking to (e.g. 'I'll have a word with your Volunteer Helper to see if he can spend more time here tomorrow') (DISCUSSION: PC2).

It is important that the member of staff should keep any promises she makes to the guest (e.g. about looking into the complaint later, having a word with the volunteer, etc.).

When speaking to the volunteer the staff member should recall that he may be unused to cleaning rooms and may have a busy schedule, including a number of rooms to clean. Once again, a sensitive and light approach is likely to be effective. Something like, 'Mr N (the guest) is particular about cleanliness. Can you spend a bit more time cleaning his room tomorrow morning?'

It is important to avoid aggressive language, including sarcasm. A comment like, 'You are meant to clean rooms, not your finger nails!' is likely to produce resentment and bad feeling all round.

 PRACTICE

USE any opportunity that arises (which could include role play) to deal with a complaint.

Listen attentively to the complaint (PC3).

Ask follow-up questions if necessary (PC4).

Respond to the complaint in a suitable tone and manner (PC2).

Deal with the complaint by taking appropriate action and by saying appropriate things to people (PC1).

 HELP
If you need further help in making or receiving complaints, turn to page 90.

 **EVIDENCE**
Assignment 5 (page 77) provides an opportunity to produce evidence of reviewing communication problems.

Dealing with a complaint by telephone

 PRACTICE

THE principles of dealing with a complaint are the same whether it is made face to face, or over the phone.

Review the last example. Summarise the principles of dealing with a complaint.

Guidance

Certain kinds of human behaviour often give rise to similar behaviour in other people. If you talk to someone angrily, there is a good chance that the other person will react angrily. The Catering Manager may be affronted at the accusation that a guest's diet has been ignored. A natural human reaction may be to flatly deny the accusation. However, this reaction, though understandable, would probably make matters worse. Therefore, it is a good idea to *count to ten*, to take a deep breath and to react calmly, even to anger.

How do you think the Catering Manager should handle this call?

The sister of a guest phones, after the guest has returned home, to complain that the guest has been ill. The sister thinks that the cause is eating food that is unsuited to the guest's diet, which should be free from sugar. Helen Donovan takes the call and senses straight away that the caller is upset and angry.

Helen begins by listening carefully to what the caller is saying, and asking questions to make sure that she understands the situation (e.g. Who was the guest? When did he stay? What kind of diet did he request?). She makes notes of the main points.

Once she has this information she offers to take the caller's number and ring back when she has investigated the complaint. It is important that she keeps this promise.

Helen then checks the guest's booking form, which includes a section on dietary needs. It states that the guest will require a sugar-free diet. She then has a word with one of her staff, who worked closely with the guest, to find out if a sugar-free diet had been given. The staff member confirms that, to the best of her recollection, this was the case. Helen then checks the kitchen records where once again it is clearly recorded that the guest should have a sugar-free diet.

Helen is by now fairly sure that the guest was given the diet he required. However, she cannot be absolutely positive. Mistakes can be made in any organisation. She telephones the guest's sister as promised and, in a suitable tone and manner (i.e. helpful and friendly) tells her that the records have been checked and staff consulted and that there is no evidence that her brother was given the wrong diet. She suggests that there may be another explanation for the guest's illness – perhaps he is tired after the journey. Helen asks if a doctor has been consulted and discovers that they are waiting for a GP to make a home visit. Helen suggests that the GP telephone her if he wishes to check what the guest ate at Francis House. She then expresses a wish that the guest will feel better soon and ends the conversation.

 PRACTICE

USE any opportunity that occurs to deal with a complaint by telephone. Such opportunities may not occur often so it is a good idea to reflect about how you would deal with a complaint, especially if the person phoning is upset or angry.

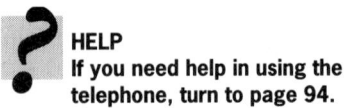

HELP
If you need help in using the
telephone, turn to page 94.

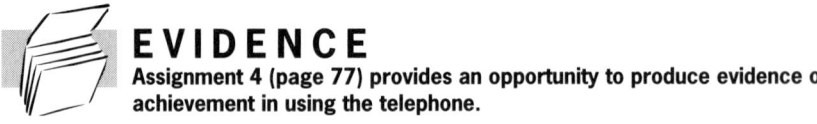

EVIDENCE
Assignment 4 (page 77) provides an opportunity to produce evidence of
achievement in using the telephone.

The Scots Fare Dinner

Craig Mackenzie, the chef at Francis House, is a Scotsman. He offers to arrange a special Scots Fare Dinner. At first, Helen Donovan is reluctant to accept, thinking that some guests may not like the food. However, Craig is persuasive, offering to take responsibility for menu planning, the purchasing of ingredients and other arrangements.

Craig begins by consulting Scots recipe books to help him focus on costs, the needs of the guests, and the time it would take kitchen staff to prepare the meal.

Once he has decided on the menu items, he checks his choices with Helen before drawing up the menu and ordering ingredients.

Whetting appetites

Craig wishes to whet guests' appetites in advance by writing a menu notice that will give a brief, tempting description of the food. The notice is intended to arouse the guests' interest so that they will look forward to the dinner.

The notice fulfils the requirements for PRODUCE WRITTEN MATERIAL at LEVEL 3: it is a non-routine document that requires careful structuring in layout and vocabulary in order to convey ideas clearly to the reader. Some of the language used is not standard English, but this is deliberate and all unfamiliar terms have been explained.

Here is Craig's menu:

Guidance

The menu notice is intended to whet people's appetites, so it needs to be more than just a naming of items. The chef hopes that, by spending time on the layout and the brief descriptions, guests will look forward with interest to his Scots Fare Dinner.

SCOTS BILL OF FARE

Some hae meat that canna eat,
And some wad eat that want it;
But we hae meat, and we can eat,
*And sae the Lord be thankit.**

Scotch Broth with Hodgils
A delicious soup of lamb cooked with barley, peas, onion, leek, cabbage, turnip and carrot. Served with Hodgils (oatmeal dumplings).
Fresh Scots baps and butter

🖎 🖎 🖎 🖎 🖎 🖎 🖎 🖎

Arbroath Smokies
A traditional, mouth-watering smoked haddock, served with pepper and butter.

🖎 🖎 🖎 🖎 🖎 🖎 🖎 🖎

Traditional Scots Haggis
Piped in by a kilted Highlander

Fair fa your honest, sonsie face
Great chieftain o' the puddin race! †

Lean mutton cooked with onion, oatmeal and cayenne. Served with tatties and neeps (potatoes and turnips to Sassenachs)‡

or

Kingdom of Fife Pie
Rabbit cooked with nutmeg and white wine. Served in a puff pastry case, accompanied by buttered peas and potatoes.

Athol Brose
A delicious pudding of oatmeal, cream and whisky.

or

Drambuie Cream
A wine jelly, served with Drambuie Cream

✄ ✄ ✄ ✄ ✄ ✄ ✄ ✄

Gaelic Coffee

✄ ✄ ✄ ✄ ✄ ✄ ✄ ✄

* An old Scottish prayer before meals:
   Some have food that cannot eat it,
   Some would like to eat but have no food;
   But we have food, and we can eat,
   And so God be thanked

† *Good befall your honest, pleasing face*
   Great chieftain of the pudding race!
‡ Saxons i.e. English people

Using images: a sketch

To illustrate the menu Craig asks a volunteer with a flair for art to draw a picture of a kilted Scottish piper. The image will be at LEVEL 3 (because it illustrates a LEVEL 3 document). The image is relevant to a Scots Fare Dinner (PC1); suits the purpose of giving the menu notice visual impact (PC2); and is used at an appropriate place in the menu – next to the reference to the kilted Highlander (PC3).

▶ PRACTICE

YOU may have to draw up a menu, or may decide to enliven an existing menu by improving its layout and/or the wording.

There are other occasions when you may wish to stir interest by writing short descriptions. Many events (e.g. a disco, a play, a sports fixture) may need a notice that is both pleasing to the eye and informative.

Take the opportunity to use images to support your writing.

HELP
If you need help in using layout, turn to page 104. If you need help in using images, turn to page 117.

EVIDENCE
Assignment 16 (page 79) provides an opportunity to produce evidence of achievement in using layout effectively.

A memo about smoking

Helen Donovan receives complaints from a number of guests that people, including volunteers, are smoking in no-smoking areas of the dining room.

She decides to write a memo to all the waiting staff asking them to try to ensure that this does not re-occur. However, as Francis House is a holiday centre and she does not want staff to treat smokers heavy-handedly, she decides to include a little advice about how staff should handle incidents of smoking.

Here is Helen's memo:

FRANCIS HOUSE

MEMO

TO: All staff
FROM: Helen Donovan, Catering Manager
DATE: 11 June
SUBJECT: Smoking in the Dining Room

I am sure that you are aware that from time to time guests, and even volunteers, smoke in no-smoking areas. This can be uncomfortable for non-smokers, some of whom have respiratory problems.

If you see anybody smoking in a no-smoking area please speak to them quietly. State that it is a no-smoking area and ask them politely to stop smoking or move to a smoking area.

Thank you for your help.

Guidance

The memo is a routine document for a manager to write (and is directed at people who will be familiar with the subject). It fulfils the requirements of PRODUCE WRITTEN MATERIAL at LEVEL 2: it includes only relevant information (PC1); it is legible (PC2); it uses standard conventions of spelling, punctuation and grammar (PC3); it is in an appropriate format – memo (PC4) with the information structured clearly and in a non-threatening style (PC5).

 PRACTICE

USE any opportunity that presents itself to write a *tactful* memo or letter that you think is suitable in content and style.

 HELP
If you need help with any aspect of writing, turn to page 97.

 **EVIDENCE**
Assignment 9 (page 78) provides an opportunity to produce evidence of achievement in writing a memo.

Using images: sketches and symbols

Helen decides to reinforce smoking rules in areas where food is eaten by putting up new No Smoking notices. She purchases standard notices to display and, in addition, designs a more friendly notice.

Here is her version of a No Smoking notice:

 PRACTICE

USE any opportunity that presents itself to design a notice that will be eye catching, non-offensive and will have the effect of making a point clearly.

You should try to use images that clearly illustrate the points being made (PC1); are suited to the audience (PC2); and that are used at appropriate times and places (PC3).

 HELP
If you need help in using images, turn to page 117.

 **EVIDENCE**
Assignment 16 (page 79) provides an opportunity to produce evidence of achievement in designing a notice.

A handout for staff

Kitchens are potential fire risk areas and Helen Donovan wishes to bring this to the attention of all staff, including volunteers. Busy staff may not have time to stop and read a notice, so she decides to give each person a handout.

Here is Helen's handout to staff. It is a non-routine document, on a subject that some staff may know little about. Consequently it is a LEVEL 3 document:

Guidance

A handout should be as brief as possible; and should be set out in a way that makes the information very clear. Numbering and lettering can be used to emphasise meaning. Other devices include paragraphing, indenting, underlining, using **bold**, using *italics*, etc.

IMPORTANT
PLEASE READ – FIRE PREVENTION IN THE KITCHEN

Every week there are serious fires in kitchens. Many of these result in death or serious injury.

PREVENTION OF FIRE

1) Kitchen Equipment
   (a) All equipment must be switched off after use.
   (b) Fryers — check debris build-up after every session.

2) Fire-Fighting Equipment & Procedure
   (a) Familiarise yourself with the fire fighting equipment:
      i) blanket for smothering flames
      ii) CO2 foam — for use on live electrical equipment or burning liquid fires
      iii) Water extinguisher — for use on paper, textiles and similar fires
         Do not use on liquid fires or live electrical equipment
      iv) First Aid Box (unclip from the wall before opening)
   (b) Familiarise yourself with the exit routes to be used in the event of serious fire.

Remember that smoke kills

 PRACTICE

USE any opportunity that presents itself to write a handout or notice that makes the meaning very clear to the reader. It is important that the document is accurate and relevant (PC1); legible and clear (PC2); uses standard conventions of spelling, punctuation and grammar (PC3); and presents the information in a structure and style that will help the audience's understanding (PC5).

When dealing with complex subjects, it is especially important that the layout of the document and the language used help the reader to understand.

HELP
If you need help in writing, turn to page 97.

 **EVIDENCE**
Assignment 12 (page 78) provides an opportunity to produce evidence of achievement in producing a handout.

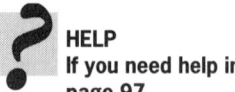 **Reading a complex document**

Guidance

Reading is not a one-gear activity. Effective and efficient reading involves finding the appropriate books or articles; and then reading them at different speeds, depending on whether you are searching for relevant information, or reading more closely.

Helen Donovan is studying for a professional qualification in Hospitality and Catering Management and, as part of her course, has to write a report on 'The Meaning of Hospitality'. She has done some background research and borrowed a book entitled *The Management of Hospitality*.

She began by looking at the contents page for a chapter that seemed relevant and saw one entitled 'Hospitality in Hospitals', which she thought might have something relevant to say about the environment in which she works.

She *scanned* through the chapter until she came to a sub-heading 'Hospitality'. Slowing down, she *skimmed* the text until she came to the following passage which seemed particularly relevant to her needs. She read the passage quite slowly:

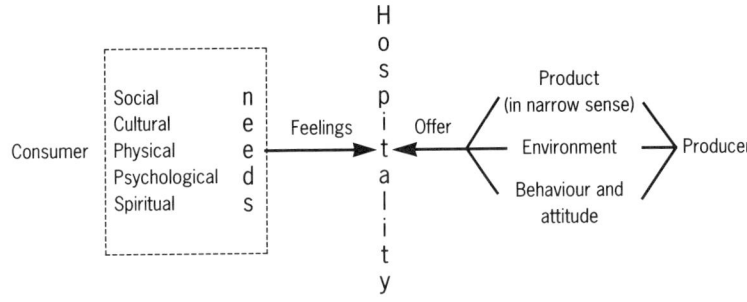

It is clear that depending on the needs and aims of the consumer, hospitality experiences (f(H)) will be based on different combinations of product (P), environment (E) and behaviour (B) and that there are even differences in the elements themselves. We can show this as an equation f(H) = aP + bE + cB.

A fast-food restaurant can be as hospitable as a first- class restaurant, depending on the aims and goals of the consumer at that time. There are consumers who feel completely at ease in a luxurious restaurant by candlelight with three waiters in black around the table. While others would be horrified – they prefer a cosy bar with soft music or a discotheque. In all these situations, however, consumers are called 'guests' and this is in contrast with situations where consumers are mostly interested in the product in a narrow sense (customers) or behaviour and attitude (clients).

(Ewout Cassee & Rudolf Reuland, 1983, *The Management of Hospitality*,
Pergamon Press)

Helen needed to consider some of the language in the passage carefully: what is meant by the 'cultural needs' of clients? How can the hospitality industry cater for people's 'spiritual needs'? What are the shades of different meanings of 'client', 'customer' and 'guest'? She thought about these terms and talked over coffee with a fellow member of the course who was struggling with similar ideas.

Later, Helen had to decide if there were points in the passage that she could make use of in her report, even if she did not necessarily agree with them. Here is her summary of the main points:

- People have a variety of needs in seeking hospitality.
- The hospitality industry offers three things: products, places, and staff.
- The industry should try to meet people's needs, whether as customers (for products), clients (to be treated with consideration), or guests (staying temporarily under someone else's roof).

▶ PRACTICE

WHEN you research material for a presentation or a report, be prepared to search for relevant materials (PC1); study the contents and index pages for potentially relevant parts; scan and skim through material searching for relevant passages; read these more slowly, making notes of the relevant information (PC2). If necessary, use appropriate sources of reference to clarify your understanding (PC3); and then finally, summarise the material extracted (PC4).

HELP
If you need help to read effectively, turn to page 123.

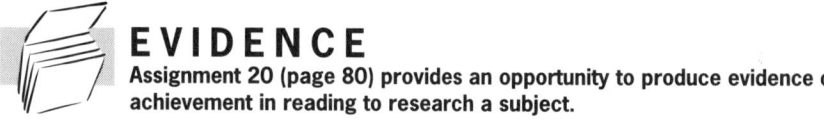

EVIDENCE

Assignment 20 (page 80) provides an opportunity to produce evidence of achievement in reading to research a subject.

4   As healthy as can be

The staff at Francis House have to help create and maintain a holiday atmosphere, while looking after the health of guests, some of whom are very ill. The communication skills that they use include:

- ▶ giving advice to guests and volunteers
- ▶ dealing tactfully with sensitive situations
- ▶ using the telephone to obtain information
- ▶ writing a variety of documents, including forms, memos and reports
- ▶ using images to monitor the health of guests
- ▶ reading and responding to a variety of documents, from diet sheets to books

Making a presentation

Guidance

Adequate preparation for a presentation is very important. This entails carrying out background research, if necessary; judging the nature of the audience (e.g. group size, age, attention span, previous knowledge, etc.); and planning the presentation accordingly.

As part of the activities at Francis House, the Senior Nurse, Anil Pradhan, and one of the care assistants, give a light-hearted talk and demonstration about Diet and Keeping Fit. Guests (even those in wheelchairs) and their helpers are invited to attend, wearing loose clothing so that they can join in.

Background reading

Anil did some background reading. He *skimmed* through an appropriately titled book, *Healthy Eating*, and came across the following passage:

> NACNE recommends a 50 per cent increase in fibre consumption, from 20 to 30 gm per day, and the simplest way of achieving this target is to eat more unrefined plant foods – cereals, vegetables, fruits and nuts – and fewer processed products.
>
> The sliced white loaf provides a good illustration of both the attractive selling points and nutritional shortcomings of refined, convenience foods. It is ready-cut, perfect for making sandwiches and toast, and lacks that nasty habit of going stale overnight. It also lacks up to two-thirds of the fibre found in wholemeal bread, as well as a large proportion of the B vitamins, and the minerals potassium, magnesium and zinc.
>
> A traditional dough simply consists of flour, water, yeast and a little salt. In order to achieve the desired consistency and shelf-life, a convenience loaf also contains an average of 15–16 additives, making British bread 'the most chemically treated in Western Europe'.
>
> (Rob Silverstone, 1990, *Healthy Eating*, Macmillan)

Guidance

When you come across a puzzling term in a book or article, it is sometimes necessary to skim back through the document, because standard practice is to explain unusual terms when they are used for the first time.

This passage is at LEVEL 3 because it is about complex matters. Anil understood most of it, except that he had not heard of NACNE. He turned to the index of the book but could find no reference to it. Skimming back through the book, to see if there was an earlier reference, he soon discovered that the initials stand for 'The National Advisory Committee on Nutrition Education'.

Anil then decided whether there were points in the passage that he should cover in the presentation. He decided that the main point, that British people should eat much more fibre, was important and needed to be included. He also thought that the example of the white loaf would help to give their audience a clearer idea of what is wrong with processed foods. He summarised these points in note form.

PRACTICE

WHEN you read background materials for reports and presentations, it is often a wise strategy to scan through until you find something relevant; then skim-read more closely; and finally study particular passages that you think will be of use. Try to have a clear question or focus in mind when you read a book – it will help you to read efficiently.

HELP
If you need help to read efficiently, turn to page 123.

EVIDENCE

Assignment 20 (page 80) provides an opportunity to produce evidence of achievement in reading to research a subject, and Assignment 13 (page 78) provides an opportunity to produce evidence of writing a report.

The main purposes of the presentation about Diet and Keeping Fit are to be informative and entertaining, so the staff take care to enliven the talk with humour, to invite questions and contributions, and to design the activities so that everyone who wishes to take part can join in.

An outline plan for the presentation may look like this:

> a) Topic: you are what you eat. Talk about the importance of particular foods: quality & quantity.
> Tell a food joke: e.g. the chicken suggested to the pig that they make bacon and eggs for the farmer's breakfast. 'Ah,' said the pig, who wasn't so sure, 'you would only be involved, whereas I would be fully committed'.
> Invite audience to tell food jokes, or amusing incidents about food.
> b) Topic: even gentle exercise helps. Demonstrate gentle stretching, Isometrics, etc.
> Guests who wish to may join in.

Making the presentation

During the presentation, the staff will: try to keep to the subject of diet and exercise (DISCUSSION PC1); fit what they say (e.g. vocabulary, tone, manner) to the audience (PC2); check that people have understood – particularly those who may have hearing difficulties (PC3); respond to the contributions of guests (PC4); and encourage everyone – even the quieter guests – to contribute to the discussion (PC5).

Using images: sketches

In order to support the main points of the presentation, the care assistant drew some simple sketches (USE IMAGES: PC1); the images suit the nature of the audience – people with poor eyesight must be able to see them (PC2); the images will be used at an appropriate time in the presentation (PC3).

The care assistant drew a food chart that could be pinned to a display board, or transferred to an overhead-projector acetate:

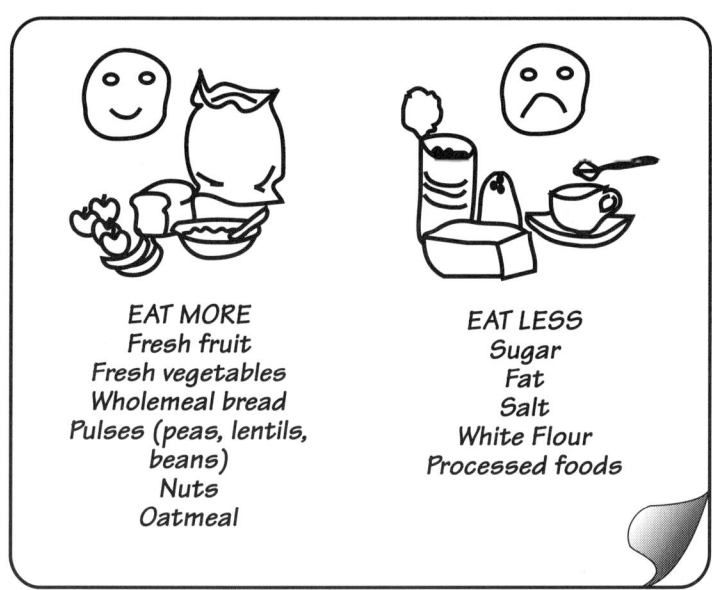

She also drew a simple cartoon to illustrate that most people, even those with disabilities, can take exercise.

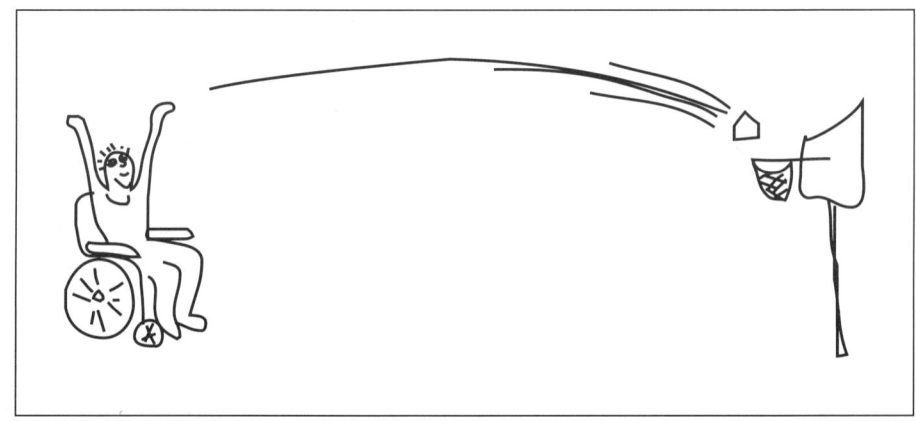

PRACTICE

E ITHER alone, or with one or more other people, give a talk or presentation on a topic of your choice. Prepare the talk with care so that the needs of the audience are considered. Try to follow all the Performance Criteria for TAKE PART IN DISCUSSIONS.

Produce suitable images to illustrate the presentation and decide in advance how and when you will use them.

Guidance

At LEVEL 2 it is important that your presentation is relevant to the subject and suited to the audience; that you listen to other people and answer their questions, clarifying any difficulties in understanding. At LEVEL 3, in addition, you should create opportunities for others to contribute, for example by inviting people to speak, or by remaining silent when appropriate.

HELP
If you need further help in making a presentation, turn to page 95.

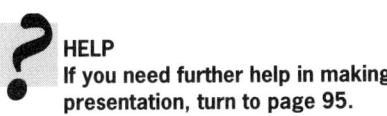 **EVIDENCE**
Assignment 3 (page 77) provides an opportunity to produce evidence of achievement in talking to a group of people.

Using the telephone

From time to time it is necessary to telephone a guest's home-carer or doctor to check details of, for example, diet or medicines.

A guest has lost a label from a tablet bottle and can't recall how many pills should be taken or how frequently. One of the nursing staff phones the guest's home-carer to try to find out.

First of all the nurse would take a good look at the size and colour of the tablets. Are they similar to any other pills the guest has? If so, the assistant must take care to distinguish them when making the telephone call.

Before making the call it is important that the nurse checks the identity of the person she wishes to speak with – this may be in the guest's file, or the guest may know.

Making the call

The nurse might follow these steps:

introduce herself;
reassure the person who receives the call that there is no emergency
    and check that she is speaking with an appropriate person;
if so, state clearly and accurately what information she seeks.

If the person she has telephoned has the information, a clear note should be made of the reply in the guest's file, and on a new label for the tablet bottle. If there is any doubt about the accuracy of the information, the nurse should refer the matter to a doctor and/or pharmacist for advice.

PRACTICE

U SE any opportunities that present themselves to make and receive telephone calls. Make brief preliminary notes of what you intend to say when making a call, and make accurate notes of what has been spoken about during a call.

Remember that, to fulfil the Performance Criteria for TAKE PART IN DISCUSSIONS:

- What you say should be relevant.

- The tone and manner in which you speak should suit the subject and the person you are speaking with.

- You should listen carefully to what the other person has to say, and ask questions to clarify anything you have not understood.

- You should respond to what the other person says in order to take forward the discussion.

Guidance

If it is necessary to scribble notes during a call, re-draft these straight away afterwards, while the information is fresh in your mind. This is especially important if you need to leave a message for another person.

 HELP
If you need more help in using the telephone, turn to page 94.

If you need more help in using the telephone, turn to page 94.

 **EVIDENCE**
Assignment 4 (page 77) provides an opportunity to produce evidence of achievement in using the telephone.

Assignment 4 (page 77) provides an opportunity to produce evidence of achievement in using the telephone.

Using images: a chart with a sketch

It became clear to the Senior Nurse of Francis House, Anil Pradhan, that some of his colleagues were nervous about making telephone calls. To help them he drew up a chart with useful advice, basing it on an acronym (a word formed from the initial letters of other words) to help them memorise the advice. The acronym is PHONE.

Guidance

The chart and accompanying sketch are intended to support the points about using the telephone. The image should be clear and relevant (PC1); suitable (PC2); and displayed in an appropriate place, e.g. beside the telephone (PC3).

```
P: Prepare:    have any necessary facts or information
               to hand;
               make sure you know who you wish to speak
               with;
               have pen and paper handy to make notes.
H: Hello:      introduce yourself and your
               organisation;
               ensure that you are speaking to an
               appropriate person.
O: Obvious:    speak clearly;
```

> make the purpose of your call *obvious*;
> *listen* carefully;
> if necessary, ask questions to *clarify* what the other person is saying.
>
> **N: Note:** make a careful and accurate note of anything important, particularly names and numbers — read these back to the other person to check their accuracy.
>
> **E: End:** end the call politely, and thank the other person for their help.

PRACTICE

CONSIDER whether information may be more effectively communicated by using a chart, or other image, that can express the information clearly and concisely

HELP
If you need help in using images, turn to page 117.

EVIDENCE

Assignment 16 (page 79) provides an opportunity to produce evidence of achievement in presenting information clearly.

The health & safety form

One of the care staff at Francis House is the Health & Safety Officer. She decides to design a simple form for staff and volunteers to use when reporting incidents and accidents. She wishes the form to be straightforward to use, and to be easy to keep on file.

A suitable form will meet the Performance Criteria for PRODUCE WRITTEN MATERIAL. It will:

- include all necessary information about a) how to complete the form, b) the accident or incident (PC1);
- be legible and clear in meaning (PC2);
- follow standard conventions of spelling, punctuation and grammar (PC3);
- be easy to use for busy staff (PC4);
- be laid out clearly and explain any unusual words (PC5).

Guidance

As the report will be filed for future reference, the Health & Safety Officer left a space at the top-right corner for a file code.

Filing Code

FRANCIS HOUSE
Form to record Incidents and Accidents

(Note: an Incident is when something potentially dangerous happened but no one was hurt, e.g. a tile fell from a roof but hit no one.
An Accident is when something actually dangerous happened, resulting in loss or injury, e.g. a tile fell from a roof on to a person or vehicle.)

Was the event an incident or accident?

Incident/Accident

Date and time of event: _____

```
Place of event:
Name of person reporting event:
                                          (Staff/Volunteer)
Please briefly describe what happened



In the event of Accident
Names of injured people:
Briefly describe the injuries:


Was First Aid given?                              Yes/No
If yes, who gave First Aid?
Was a nurse called?                               Yes/No
Was a doctor called?                              Yes/No
Was an ambulance called?                          Yes/No

Signed                          Date

TO BE COMPLETED BY THE HEALTH & SAFETY OFFICER:
What subsequent action was taken to prevent a re-
occurrence?


What further steps should be taken to improve Health &
Safety provision?

Signed                          Date
```

 **PRACTICE**

WHAT File Code system could the Health & Safety Officer use? How can the task of searching for a particular report be simplified? (The filing could be organised by, for example, date, place, seriousness.)
How would you code these reports for filing?

The Health & Safety Officer decides to use the following system to code the reports: **A** or **I** to signify whether the form records an accident or an incident; followed by * if an accident resulted in serious injury; followed by the last two digits of the year (e.g. 98 = 1998); followed by the number of the accident that year, or the number of the incident that year.

So, a file code may look like this: A*96/4.

This would show, at a glance, that the report refers to a serious accident, and that it was the fourth accident to occur in 1996.

In a filing cabinet all accidents are grouped together by year, with the most recent at the front. All incidents are grouped in the same way.

PRACTICE

ASK if you may study a copy of any standard accident report forms used at your school/college/ work. How well-designed do you think they are? Do they cover all the information that is needed? Are they reasonably easy to use? Can they be filed so that they can be found again easily?

If you can, take the opportunity to re-design a form, or to design a new form that will help to record facts simply and clearly.

HELP
If you need help in using layout when producing written material, turn to page 104.

EVIDENCE
Assignment 16 (page 79) provides an opportunity to produce evidence of achievement in using layout effectively.

The memo

Guidance

It is not necessary to sign a memo. The memo format states the subject as briefly as possible, however, it should still meet all the Performance Criteria for PRODUCE WRITTEN MATERIAL. It should:
• be accurate and include all the relevant information (PC1);
• be legible and clear (PC2) and written using standard conventions of spelling, punctuation and grammar (PC3);
• be suited to audience and purpose – the memo format should itself be suitable (PC4), and the information should be ordered to maximise the reader's understanding, by using paragraphs, numbers, letters or any suitable means of emphasising the meaning (PC5).

The Health & Safety Officer decides to send a few copies of the new Report Form to each member of staff, and to let each new volunteer have a copy. To accompany the forms the Health & Safety Officer writes a short memo, explaining how to use them.

MEMO

```
TO:        All staff and volunteers
FROM:      The Health & Safety Officer
DATE:      5 October
SUBJECT:   Use of Accident/Incident Report Forms

We are required by law to record all accidents. To
make this easier, please use the attached form, which
should be completed as soon after the event as
possible.

Thank you for your help.
```

This particular memo, which is about a straightforward administrative matter is at LEVEL 2.

PRACTICE

YOU may receive memos from time to time. Is the outline format pre-printed? If not, would it save time if it was? Is the writer clear and brief in what is stated?

Use any opportunity that occurs to write memos. Remember to keep a copy for assessment purposes.

HELP
If you need help in writing memos, turn to page 98.

EVIDENCE
Assignment 9 (page 78) provides an opportunity to produce evidence of achievement in writing memos.

Using images: charts

The Health & Safety Officer devises a simple flow chart to help staff keep in mind what to do in the event of an accident:

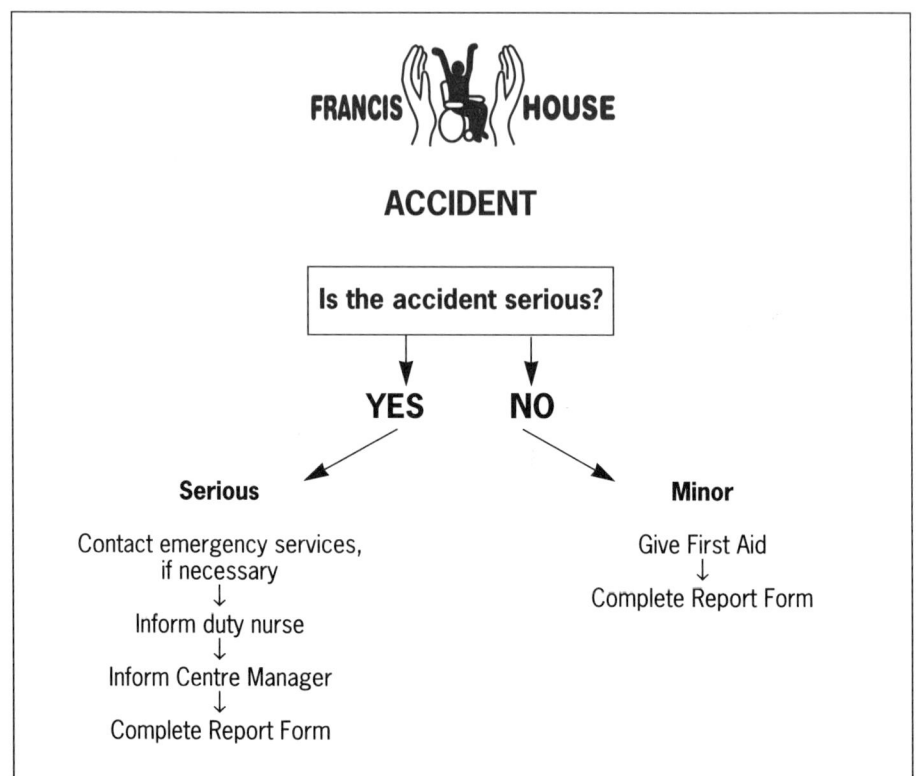

 **HELP**
If you need help to use images, turn to page 117.

EVIDENCE
Assignment 16 (page 79) provides an opportunity to produce evidence of achievement in using layout, such as a chart, to convey information clearly.

A sensitive situation

A guest who is occasionally incontinent does not reach the toilet in time and wets himself in the dining room. He is very embarrassed and says that he wishes to return home, although he has many days of his holiday left. A care assistant is with him and wishes to persuade him to stay and enjoy his holiday.

 PRACTICE

IMAGINE the sorts of embarrassing situations that could arise in a public situation with which you are familiar. How do you think they should be handled? Do you think you have the necessary skills to handle them effectively?

Guidance

You will see that this situation is at LEVEL 3. It is a *sensitive* complex situation (involving discussion with someone who is not well known to the care assistant). The care assistant needs to:
- make effective and relevant contributions (PC1);
- speak in a suitable tone and manner (PC2);
- listen attentively and respond appropriately (PC3);
- if necessary, ask questions to clarify what the guest is saying about his thoughts and feelings (PC4);
- encourage the guest to talk (PC5).

Anil Pradhan has prepared some written advice about caring for guests to be given to all staff at Francis House, including volunteers. The essence of the advice is:

At all times try to respect the guest's *dignity* and *independence.*

The care assistant, therefore, avoids behaviour that would infringe this principle. She does not laugh at what has happened, or pretend that it is completely trivial; she does not talk down to the person or attempt to deal with the issue in public.

Taking the guest to his room she helps the guest to change and make himself comfortable, as she is used to doing. While doing this she will show, by her manner and by what she says (e.g. in subject, tone and through non-verbal communication), that *she* is not embarrassed by what has happened but that she understands and respects the fact that the guest may be upset. She will be prepared to listen to what the guest has to say, and to give him time to compose himself (perhaps by leaving the guest alone while she goes to fetch him a cup of tea).

When the guest is ready to talk she will listen to his feelings and his reasons for wishing to leave – if he still wishes to do so. She may ask questions to clarify the guest's feelings and to help him express them; and she may honestly express her own view that the guest should stay, but without imposing this opinion. At the end of the discussion, the guest has a right to leave if he wishes, and this should not be challenged.

 PRACTICE

REFLECT on any situation that you have experienced that was embarrassing. How well was it handled by the people involved? It is impossible to predict when such a situation will arise but consider how you think you would feel and behave.

? HELP
If you need help in talking and listening, turn to page 87.

 **EVIDENCE**
Assignment 1 (page 77) provides an opportunity to produce evidence of achievement in taking part in one-to-one discussions.

Recording information

Guidance

Charts enable information to be conveyed in a simple visual format. They make it easier for the reader to understand the subject matter.

In this case it is important that the chart is completed accurately, and therefore it is designed for precise use.

Using images: a chart

At Francis House it is sometimes necessary for care staff to record a guest's temperature. A temperature chart enables staff, including doctors on call, to see at a glance useful information about a guest's state of health.

The chart uses two axes: the temperature, recorded in this case in degrees centigrade; and the time intervals between recordings.

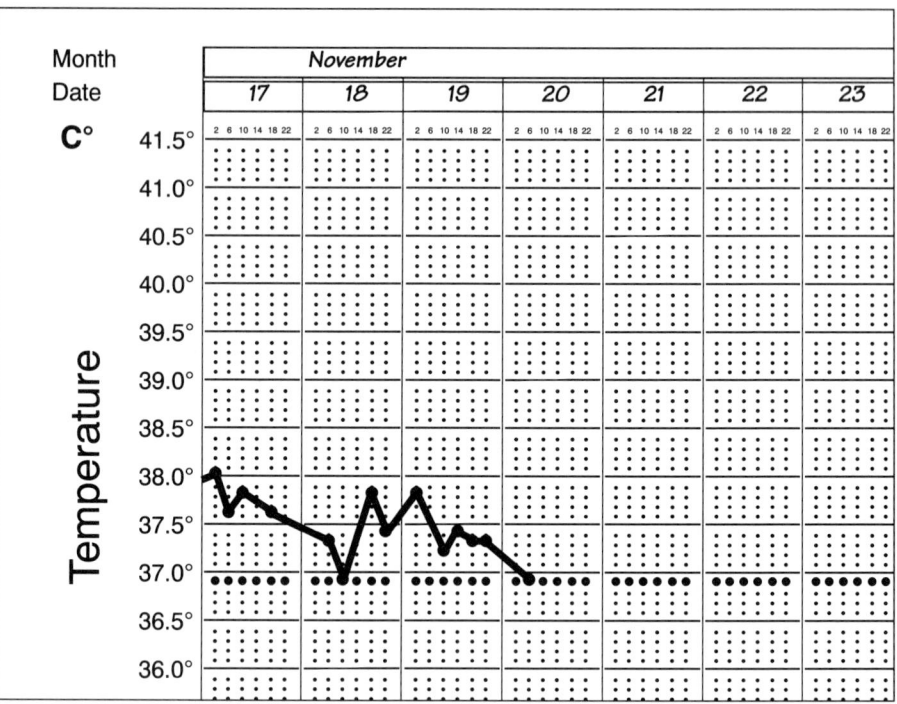

HELP
If you need help in using charts, turn
to page 119.

EVIDENCE
Assignment 17 (page 79) provides an opportunity to produce evidence of
achievement in presenting statistical information.

The paperwork of a meeting

The care staff meet every month to discuss any issues that individuals
think are important.

The meetings are chaired by the Senior Nurse, Anil Pradhan, and one of
the care assistants acts as Secretary by taking notes so that, following the
meeting, minutes can be circulated.

Anil circulates a notice in advance so that people can indicate any issues
they wish to be discussed. Here is a typical notice:

FRANCIS HOUSE

```
The next monthly meeting of care staff will be held on
_____. Please let Anil have any items for the
agenda by _____.
```

Once he has received the replies, Anil writes the agenda and circulates it
in advance so that people can think about the issues.

FRANCIS HOUSE

The next monthly meeting of care staff will be held on
_____ in the Staff Room.

AGENDA

1) Apologies for absence
2) Minutes of the last meeting
3) Matters arising
4) Guests' medicines on outings
5) Cleaning of bedrooms
6) Advice to volunteers about physical care of guests
7) Any other business
8) Date of next meeting

Guidance

This is a typical agenda structure for meetings (in businesses, schools, colleges, and government departments) that deals logically with the business of the meeting.

The minutes

After the meeting the person who took the notes (usually the Secretary, but often another person, sometimes the Chair) should write them up for circulation to all those who attended the meeting.

Here are the minutes of the meeting of care staff:

FRANCIS HOUSE

Minutes of the monthly meeting of care staff held on
_____ in the Staff Room.

Present: [the names of all those who attended,
indicating who chaired the meeting]

1) Apologies for absence: [the names of any people
   who could not attend and who sent their apologies]
2) Minutes of the last meeting: the minutes of the
   last meeting were accepted as a true record.
3) Matters arising: Anil reported on his meeting with
   the builders about improving wheelchair access to
   the garden pavilion.
4) Guests' medicines on outings: it was agreed that
   all guests' medicines should be clearly marked and
   allocated to suitably named containers. A red
   plastic Drug Box is provided to store the
   containers and this should be returned to the duty
   room after the outing.
ACTION: ALL CARE STAFF
5) Cleaning of bedrooms: cleaning staff are asked to
   ensure that, when setting up rooms for guests on
   Saturdays, all headboards are wiped clean, and
   that the mattresses are wiped with a solution of
   disinfectant before turning them ready for the
   next guests.
ACTION: ALL CLEANING STAFF
6) Advice to volunteers about physical care of
   guests: it was agreed that the Senior Nurse will
   draw up guidance for volunteers that will be sent
   to them in advance.

Guidance

This is a typical set of minutes from a meeting. Minutes should be as brief as possible, while being accurate and representing fairly what has been discussed. It is particularly important that, if action is to be taken, it is clear what this will be and who will carry it out.

```
ACTION: ANIL PRADHAN
7)  Any other business: staff were reminded that they
    should wear name badges at all times while on
    duty.
8)  The next meeting will take place on _____.
```

These minutes are at LEVEL 2 for PRODUCE WRITTEN MATERIAL because they deal with routine matters and are written for people who will be familiar with the subject matter. However, some minutes may be at LEVEL 3, if they deal with complex and/or sensitive issues; or are written for people unfamiliar with the subject.

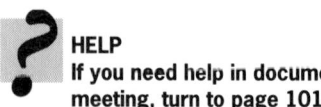

PRACTICE

USE any opportunity that arises to write the minutes of a meeting. For example, you may attend a meeting and offer to take the minutes in order to gain practice. Take a look at the minutes of other meetings (preferably of meetings you have attended). Are they accurate but brief? Do they make plain what action should be taken, and by whom?

HELP
If you need help in documenting a meeting, turn to page 101.

EVIDENCE
Assignment 7 (page 78) provides an opportunity to produce evidence of achievement in writing the minutes of a meeting.

Advice to volunteers about physical care

Following the monthly meeting of care staff (item 6), Anil writes some advice for volunteers about the physical care of disabled guests. He wishes the advice to be brief (otherwise it may not be read), accurate (otherwise difficulties may arise that the advice is designed to avoid), and clear.

In other words, he follows the Performance Criteria for PRODUCE WRITTEN MATERIAL at LEVEL 3.

Here is his advice, on a single sheet to be sent to volunteers:

PHYSICAL CARE may be your main concern before you arrive at the Centre, because it may be a new experience and because it involves helping people with intimate and very personal needs.

WE DO NOT EXPECT ALL VOLUNTEERS TO FEEL INSTANTLY AT EASE BUT IT MAY HELP TO CONSIDER SOME ASPECTS OF CARE IN THIS WAY:

All of us need to eat, drink, wash, dress, use the toilet, and get in and out of bed every day of our lives. Some people, because of their disabilities, need help to carry out these basic daily activities. We are not asking you to do anything unusual, or anything that most of us don't take for granted.

Obviously helping with SOMEONE ELSE'S NEEDS will be a new experience, that will demand more thought and effort. BUT PLEASE REMEMBER THESE ARE BASIC NEEDS. It is important that you try to help our guests without fuss, and avoid making them feel that these ordinary daily needs are a problem and an embarrassment.

Guidance

The information is accurate and relevant (PC1), The text is legible and written in clear English (PC2) following standard conventions of spelling, punctuation and grammar (PC3). The format – one sheet – suits the audience and purpose – it is likely to be read (PC4). The layout and language used help to make meaning clear (PC5).

Here are some useful hints to consider when helping guests:

- Always ask the guests how they normally do things, and as far as possible carry out their wishes.
- Be aware that **skin care** is very important for most people with disabilities, and can cause serious problems if not tended to properly, so always wash or bathe guests carefully and thoroughly.
- Let the guests choose which clothes they wish to wear, and ensure that clean clothing is available when needed.
- Be patient with people, particularly where communication may be difficult or time consuming.
- Don't take away the guest's independence for the sake of time or convenience to yourself.
- Consider the smaller personal needs such as cleaning teeth, shaving, combing hair and make-up, even assisting with nose blowing. These can easily be forgotten as they are so often done without really thinking.

AT ALL TIMES TRY TO RESPECT THE GUEST'S DIGNITY AND INDEPENDENCE AND YOU WON'T GO FAR WRONG.

PRACTICE

USE any opportunity you have to write a letter, article, report or other form of writing that deals with a sensitive issue. Try to ensure that the tone of the writing is suitable (i.e. it *sounds* right – clear without being intimidating). Choose a format that is appropriate. Lay out the writing in a way that will help the reader's understanding. Highlight main points, use indentation, asterisks, numbers or other means of indicating main points. Remember that the reader may be unfamiliar with at least some aspects of the subject matter.

HELP
If you need help with any aspect of writing, turn to page 97.

EVIDENCE

Assignment 12 (page 78) provides an opportunity to produce evidence of achievement in producing a handout of information.

Guidance

In order to help you understand what you have read, it is sometimes helpful to summarise the main points for someone else. This focuses your thoughts.

Reading the advice

Anil Pradhan asked a volunteer to read the advice he had written about physical care, to check that he had made his points clearly.

The volunteer read the document, which is at LEVEL 2 because it is straightforward in the context, and Anil is ready to help him if necessary. The volunteer liked the layout and thought that the use of bold lettering, and a list of do's and don'ts made the points easier to follow. Anil asked him to summarise what he thought the main point was.

The volunteer said that it was that people should remember that disabled guests sometimes need help with simple, everyday things that volunteers may sometimes overlook, because they are such ordinary needs; or volunteers may even disparage guests for needing such basic help. He added that he liked the reminder to respect guests' dignity and independence, but was not sure what the term 'independence' meant.

Anil asked him what he thought the term meant. A discussion followed in which they agreed that the term, in this context, means that disabled people should be given every opportunity to care for themselves – help should be given only when the disabled person needs it, and not simply to suit the needs of the helper, for example, to get something done quickly.

 PRACTICE

WHEN you read documents, be prepared to discuss them with colleagues and tutors so that you can all reach a better understanding of what has been written. In this way you will be helped to meet the Performance Criteria for READ AND RESPOND TO MATERIALS:

- select and read materials for a purpose (in this case to obtain information) – PC1

- extract the necessary information (in this case about helping disabled people) – PC2

- check your understanding (e.g. with a colleague or friend) – PC3

- summarise the information – PC4

? HELP
If you need help in reading effectively, turn to page 123.

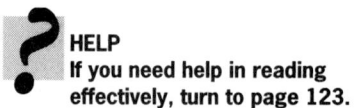 **EVIDENCE**
Assignment 21 (page 80) provides an opportunity to produce evidence of achievement in using appropriate sources of reference.

Using images: diagrams

In order to help volunteers to lift guests without injuring themselves Francis House has obtained permission to reproduce some diagrams from a book of techniques. Here is an example:

THROUGH ARM LIFT

(1) People who are unable to stand, i.e., those who will need a total lift from a to b. The most commonly used lift is the **THROUGH ARM LIFT** with a second helper lifting legs.

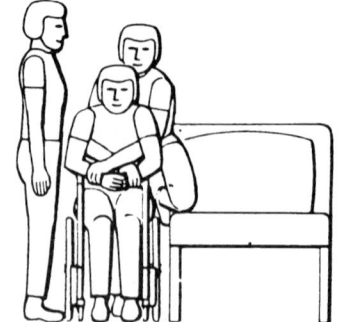

Park chair parallel to and against bed. Brakes on, near side arm-rest removed and footplates swung away.
Helper   Stand behind chair on bed side of wheelchair handles. Put bed side knee on bed, point other foot in direction of chair and bend knee slightly. Take person in a through-arm, wrist crossed-over grip.

Remember to co-ordinate the lift
Helper   Straighten supporting leg and rock weight over on to bed side knee as you lift person up and over on to bed.
Helper .   Straighten your knees and lift person up and over on to bed. If necessary, take a couple of steps forward between chair and bed.

Guidance

You can see from the illustrations that a diagram is able to show techniques that are difficult to convey by words alone. If a diagram is particularly important (for example, because it may prevent injuries) it may be preferable to use professionally produced images (with permission) rather than images that may be unclear and suit the purpose less (USE IMAGES: PC2).

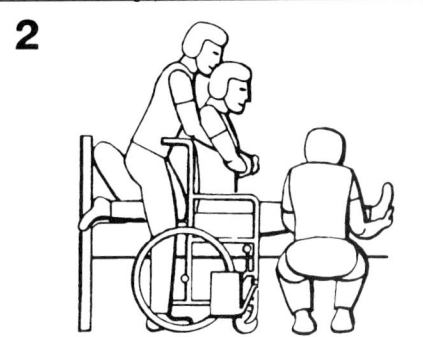

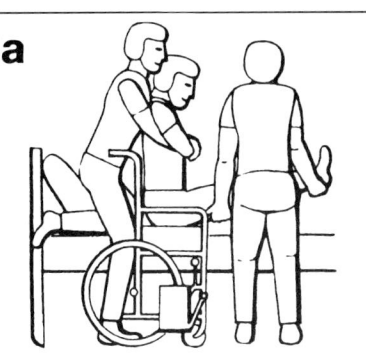

Helper   Squat down beside person's legs facing bed. Slide one hand under person's thighs and other hand under heels.

Notes

The example shows a lift from chair to bed. This basic technique is the same for bed to chair, loo or other seat (except both feet will be on the ground). It can also be used to correct a person's sitting position.

The taller helper should be *behind* the guest.

Other techniques may be preferred by the guests, so please remember to ask them first or *consult a member of staff if you are unsure*.

PRACTICE   USE any opportunity that presents itself to make use of professionally produced images to support your writing or presentations.

HELP
If you need help to use images, turn to page 117.

EVIDENCE
Assignment 15 (page 79) provides an opportunity to produce evidence of achievement in using professionally produced images.

Reading the diagrams

Anil asked a volunteer to read and comment on the Through-Arm Lift diagrams, to check that she found them reasonably easy to follow. The diagrams are at LEVEL 3 for the volunteer, because the subject is complex and non-routine for her. She needs to extract the necessary information from the images (READ AND RESPOND: PC2) and check the meaning of anything she does not understand (PC3).

The volunteer studied the diagrams and the accompanying text for a few minutes and asked Anil what 'Straighten supporting leg and rock weight over on to bed side knee' meant. Anil explained as much as he could but added that the volunteer would need to practise the technique to fully understand all the instructions.

Anil then asked the volunteer to attempt to identify and summarise the main points of the diagrams (PC4). The volunteer thought they were that:

1) two people should work in unison to lift an adult;

2) the helpers' backs should be kept straight;

3) helpers should bend from the knees and lift with the thigh muscles;

4) helpers should use smooth, careful movements.

Anil agreed with these responses and was pleased that the diagram could be understood without great difficulty. He then asked the volunteer to assist him in lifting a guest. The volunteer showed that she was able to follow the advice in the diagrams.

 PRACTICE

WHEN you read material that makes use of images, ensure that you understand the points they are making, and if there is anything you do not understand, check with an appropriate source of reference (e.g. person, dictionary, encyclopedia, etc.).

 HELP
If you need help in reading and understanding images, turn to page 122.

 **EVIDENCE**
Assignment 23 (page 80) provides an opportunity to produce evidence of achievement in showing understanding of images.

EVIDENCE OPPORTUNITIES

Gathering evidence of achievement

Evidence of achievement may be gathered from:

- previous education and experience;
- work carried out for any GNVQ or NVQ unit;
- work carried out on any other education programme (e.g. GCSE, A level, A/S level);
- experience outside education (e.g. in a part-time job, a hobby, a club, etc.).

Assignments and projects

In practice, on a GNVQ programme, you will carry out assignments and projects that cover a number of elements, or even a number of units, simultaneously. For example, you may read books that contain images, in order to prepare a handout that you will give to people as part of a presentation. The elements of Communication are inter-related, like this:

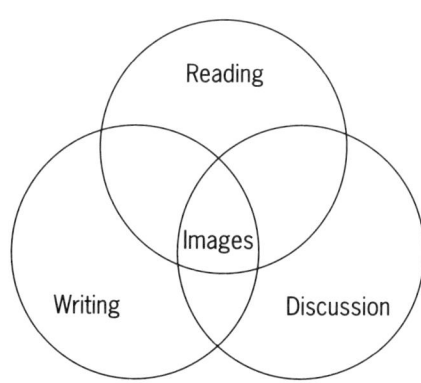

For the purpose of assessment, however, it may be necessary to break down what you have done, in order to show that you have satisfied the performance criteria for the particular elements of Communication.

Cover all relevant performance criteria

Whatever the source of evidence, it is essential that it covers all the relevant performance criteria for an element of Communication. For example, if you cite a discussion you took part in as evidence for ELEMENT 2.1 OR 3.1: TAKE PART IN DISCUSSIONS, it is necessary to show that you have satisfied *all* the relevant criteria – you can't claim that your contributions have been relevant (PC 1) if, for instance, you have not listened to and understood what other people have said (PC 3). If the criteria are applicable to a particular activity, you must satisfy them all, and show evidence that you have done so.

Cover all parts of range

The range statements show, for each element, what sorts of subjects, audiences and situations you must deal with in communicating.

Audience

In order to show that you can use a variety of styles of speaking, writing and using images to suit the needs of different people, it is necessary to communicate with a range of audiences:

At level 2 and 3:
- people familiar with the subject who know you
- people familiar with the subject who do not know you

At level 3:
- people unfamiliar with the subject who know you
- people unfamiliar with the subject who do not know you

Record the type of audience for each activity to ensure that you cover the range necessary.

In the assignments that follow, it is sometimes clear what kind of audience is involved, and sometimes it is up to you to involve people from outside your group, in order to ensure that you have experience of communicating with different audiences.

Presenting your evidence to an assessor

At the beginning of your GNVQ programme you should make sure that you are clear about who will assess your work. Often you will be taught by a number of people, and it is the responsibility of those teaching you to make plain to you the arrangements for assessment. **If you are not clear, ask.**

The more well organised you are in presenting evidence of achievement, the more you will help assessors to make reliable judgements about your work. This in turn will help you to learn and to develop.

Take part in discussions

Evidence of achievement should be given in ways that enable an assessor to make a reliable judgement. For you to say, 'I covered ELEMENT 2.1: TAKE PART IN DISCUSSIONS by talking to customers in a shop last Saturday', without actually showing some evidence (e.g. a letter from the manager that refers to how you covered the performance criteria, and a tape recording of you talking to customers) makes it impossible for an assessor to make a judgement.

In practice, it is often easier to gather evidence when the assessor is actually present, i.e. during your GNVQ course, when activities and projects are set up specifically for you to practise and show what you can do. So, for example, you may be observed by an assessor while you are taking part in discussions.

Produce written material and produce images

Evidence of writing, and using images, can be collected in a portfolio of documents. It must be evident that this is all your own work, that it shows coverage of all the performance criteria, and that it covers the range.

The portfolio should contain a variety of formats of writing (e.g. letters, reports, notes); and a variety of images (e.g. photographs, charts, sketches – some of which you will have produced yourself for a particular purpose).

Read and respond to materials

Evidence of reading may be more difficult to gather, and it may be necessary to keep a log of all books and articles that you have read, that also shows how you have *used* and *responded* to your reading.

Liaise with an assessor before you embark on your reading; keep careful records of everything you read; make notes of the key points you discover; keep a careful record of how you have used your reading (e.g. to write a report, prepare a presentation, etc.).

Don't forget that you need to gather evidence of reading and responding to images (e.g. charts, graphs, tables, maps) as well as written materials.

Summary of how to record achievement

Some of the ways you may gather evidence of achievement are by keeping:

- a portfolio of written material (letters, memos, reports, etc.);
- a portfolio of images used;
- a log of people spoken to, perhaps divided into telephone calls, discussions with individuals, and presentations to groups of people;
- a record of all books and articles read, and how you used this reading in your assignments, etc.

Whatever types of recording you use, it is essential to show how the *performance criteria* for the particular *level* you wish to achieve have been satisfied, together with the requirements of *range* (e.g. that you have spoken with and written to the full range of audiences).

Suggestions for assignments

Here are suggestions for assignments to improve your performance in Communication and to help you build a portfolio of evidence of achievement. These assignments may supplement those you will complete as part of your GNVQ course.

The assignments are organised in six sections:

- four sections contain assignments that relate to each of the four elements – so that you may focus on developing a particular skill (pages 77–80);
- two sections contain assignments that cover a number of elements for LEVEL 2 (pages 81–83) and for LEVEL 3 (pages 83–85).

When you have completed an assignment successfully, tick the box and write in the date, as a reminder.

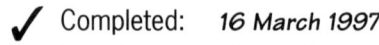
✓ Completed: *16 March 1997*

Take care to record your achievement in the documents provided on your GNVQ course.

Assignments for Element 1: Take part in discussions (levels 2 and 3)

Level: whether a discussion is at LEVEL 2 or LEVEL 3 depends on the complexity of the subject and the nature of the audience. Complex, non-routine subjects, requiring careful use of language to make meaning clear, and discussions with people unfamiliar with the subject are at LEVEL 3. If you are in doubt, consult the assessor in advance.

1. Take part in one-to-one discussions

Completed:

Use any opportunity that occurs on your GNVQ course to take part in discussions with other people. Review the performance criteria for discussions and try to ensure that you listen and respond, as well as speak.

If an assessor is not present, you may have to record the meeting on audio or video tape to provide sufficient evidence of your contributions (see *Recording the voice* on page 96).

2. Attend a meeting

Completed:

Use any opportunity that occurs on your GNVQ course or in your outside life to attend a meeting with one or more people (e.g. with a teacher, job-placement employer, local Careers Officer).

Prepare for the meeting in advance by making some notes. Contribute appropriately and review your speaking and listening against the Performance Criteria for TAKE PART IN DISCUSSIONS.

If an assessor is not present, you may have to record the meeting on audio tape or video tape to provide sufficient evidence of your contributions (see *Recording the voice* on page 96).

Make notes after the meeting to summarise the main points that were discussed. If the meeting is a formal one that is minuted, obtain a copy of the minutes.

3. Speak to a group of people

Completed:

Use an opportunity that occurs on your course or in your private life to give a talk to a group of people.

The talk should last no more than 10 minutes and should be prepared by making brief notes (to jog your memory, *not* to read from). It may be illustrated by the use of appropriate images. Leave time after your talk for a discussion of some of the issues raised. Adjust what you say to how much the audience will know about the subject.

Retain your preparatory notes for the talk. The talk should either be attended by someone who can assess you, or should be video- or audio-taped so that it can be assessed later (see *Recording the voice* on page 96).

Obtain feedback

It would be useful, if possible, to ask your audience to complete an *Evaluation Sheet* at the end of your talk (see page 96).

4. Use the telephone

Completed:

Keep a written record of all telephone calls you make that may satisfy all the Performance Criteria for the level you require:

- keep the notes you make to prepare the call;
- keep the notes you make during and after the call;
- make a tape recording of your speaking during two or three calls to use as evidence that you satisfy the Performance Criteria for ELEMENT 2.1 or 3.1 (see *Recording the voice* on page 96).

5. Review communication problems

Completed:

During discussions there will be occasions when people do not communicate harmoniously or effectively – for example, there may be disagreements; or a complaint may be made or responded to inappropriately; or someone may give a talk that is not understood by the audience. You may learn from these occasions. Consult *The Help Section* on *Take part in discussions* (pages 87–97) and review the ineffective discussion. What can you learn from what happened?

Write a brief report.

Assignments for Element 2: Produce written material (levels 2 and 3)

Level: whether written material is at LEVEL 2 or LEVEL 3 depends on the complexity of the subject and the nature of the audience. Complex, non-routine subjects, requiring careful use of structure and style to make meaning clear, and materials produced for people unfamiliar with the subject, are at LEVEL 3. If you are in doubt, consult the assessor in advance.

6. Notes for a meeting

Completed:

Prepare notes for a meeting. Consider the subject of the meeting and the nature of the audience (e.g. how much they will know about the subject). It may be a good idea to include an image (e.g. a diagram, a table, a graph) in order to be able to support a point you wish to make. Keep the notes in a portfolio, together with a record of the meeting.

7. Minutes of a meeting

Completed:

Agree to take notes at a meeting (e.g. an assignment planning meeting; a club meeting) and write the minutes of the meeting, following the guidance given in *The Help Section* (page 104).

8. A flipchart sheet

Completed:

Produce a single flipchart sheet, illustrated by a suitable image, to display as part of a presentation.

You may have to research the subject (e.g. by consulting people; reading material). Make sure that the sheet is legible, even from the back of the room. Write it in a way that makes the subject as clear as possible to the readers, especially if they are unfamiliar with the subject. Check the spelling, punctuation and grammar.

9. A memo

Completed:

Write a memo to a member of staff or to people on your course, confirming details of an agreement or arrangement that forms part of preparations for a group assignment.

10. Drafting and re-drafting

Completed:

When you produce a piece of written work, ask a friend to comment on it positively and then re-draft it, taking account of their comments.

11. A letter

Completed:

Write a letter to an individual you do not know, or to a firm, requesting information about a subject of direct relevance to your GNVQ. Ensure that the layout of the letter is suitable; state the subject in the opening paragraph; keep the letter as brief as possible, while covering all relevant points; check spelling, punctuation and grammar.

12. A handout

Completed:

To provide information to people (e.g. as part of a presentation, or as background to a project) produce a handout of key points. You may be able to produce some photocopies (not necessarily one per person).

13. A report

Completed:

Research a topic that is part of your GNVQ (e.g. by consulting people; reading books and articles). Make notes of any relevant material. Summarise your notes in the form of a written report, supported by images. Set out the report to a length and format agreed in advance with your tutor or assessor (e.g. use sub-headings, numbering or lettering to organise material); when you write the report, bear in mind who the audience will be, and how much they will know about the subject; check the spelling, punctuation and grammar.

14. An article

Completed:

Write a short article for a school/college/company newspaper or magazine; or for a local publication. It may be necessary to research the subject (e.g. by consulting people; reading material). Make notes of any relevant material. Summarise your notes in the form of an article, perhaps supported by images. Set out the article in a way that will maximise audience interest and understanding (bear in mind how much they will know about the subject) to a length agreed with the editor. Check spelling, punctuation and grammar.

Assignments for Element 3: Use images (levels 2 and 3)

Level: whether images are at LEVEL 2 or LEVEL 3 depends on the level of the written or spoken communication they support. If you are in doubt, consult the assessor in advance.

15. Photographs

Completed:

Take photographs (prints or slides) or reproduce professionally produced images to illustrate a talk on a subject of relevance to your GNVQ. Make sure that the pictures illustrate clearly the points you wish to make, and will be understood by the audience. Use them at an appropriate time during the talk. Ensure that the audience can see slides (even from the back of the room) or have time to examine prints. Keep a record of your images and how you used them.

16. Use layout to enhance communication

Completed:

Use layout to enhance the meaning and impact of a document (e.g. a poster, notice, leaflet or form). Use one or more images, either from source material, such as books and magazines, or that you have produced yourself to suit the particular purpose of the poster (e.g. to attract attention, arouse interest, convey information). Check the spelling of any words used. Consult other people about the effectiveness of the poster for its purpose.

17. Present statistical information

Completed:

Select a suitable image (e.g. graph, table, pie chart or bar chart, etc.) to present figures about a subject relevant to your GNVQ. Choose an image that will present the information as clearly as possible, given the subject and the particular audience (e.g. how much will they know about the subject?). Make a record of how you used the image (e.g. in written material or a discussion) and how effective it was in communicating the information.

18. A sketch

Completed:

Draw a sketch to illustrate written material or a discussion. The sketch may be very simple (e.g. using matchstick people) as long as it serves the purpose intended (e.g. to communicate information; introduce some humour; arouse people's interest). Maximise the effectiveness of the sketch by using it at an appropriate time during a discussion, or at a suitable point in a document. Keep the sketch and a record of how you used it.

19. Draw a map

Completed:

Draw a map for someone who is not familiar with the area. It should be accurate, while being straightforward to read. Give the map a sense of scale and include a few landmarks or other features to help orientate the reader. Check on its use to see that it is suitable in practice.

Assignments for Element 4: Read and respond to materials (levels 2 and 3)

Level: whether reading material is at LEVEL 2 or LEVEL 3 depends on the complexity of the subject. Complex, non-routine materials, requiring careful reading and judgement for full understanding, are at LEVEL 3. If you are in doubt, consult the assessor in advance.

20. Research in a library

Completed:

Use a library to investigate a topic of interest to you (see *The Help Section*, page 123) that is directly linked to your GNVQ, or to a hobby or other personal interest. Make notes of the information you discover, using a card index or similar system for storing and retrieving information. Record the name of each author and the title, publisher and date of publication of each book or article consulted. Remember that reading is not a one-gear activity – use contents pages and bibliographies; scan and skim, in order to extract efficiently the information you need.

21. Use appropriate sources of reference

Completed:

From time to time you will come across parts of written material that you will not understand, and you must be able to show that you can use appropriate sources of reference. At LEVEL 2, sources of reference will be provided for you; at LEVEL 3 you may have to find them yourself. Sometimes it is best to ask another person for help (e.g. a tutor, another student) and at other times you may have to consult books, such as a dictionary, thesaurus or encyclopedia. Use the reference section of a library and consult a range of reference materials. Ask a librarian for help in finding the most suitable

references. Keep a note of the sources you use and how you use them.

22. Compare newspaper reports

Completed:

When a subject of relevance to your GNVQ is in the news, study the ways in which several national newspapers deal with it.

Judge the relevance, fullness and accuracy of each newspaper's coverage and write a brief report that may be used to make a presentation to your group.

23. Understand images

Completed:

From time to time in your reading you will see images (e.g. symbols, charts, sketches) that convey information. Write notes on these to show that you have understood them.

24. Read and respond to images that present statistical information

Completed:

The reference section of most libraries contains a number of publications that present statistical information (e.g. about government departments; companies; countries) in the form of tables, graphs, charts, etc. Search for relevant statistical information on a topic connected with your GNVQ. Read the images, making notes of any information that is relevant to your purpose (e.g. to prepare for a discussion; to write a report). As with other written materials, use a card index or similar system for storing and retrieving information. Record the name of each publication with its publisher and date. Don't forget to use appropriate sources of clarification (e.g. a tutor, a librarian) to help you understand the images.

Combined assignments for level 2

Level: there is no reason why LEVEL 3 students should not complete these assignments, adding to them as appropriate to cover all the performance criteria for LEVEL 3.

25. Apply for a job

Completed:

Write your own Curriculum Vitae (CV). It does not have to be for an actual job, although it helps to have a specific job in mind that might be feasible to apply for (have a look through local and national newspapers, or magazines relevant to your GNVQ area, to get an idea of a relevant job to apply for). Read about writing a CV in *The Help Section* (page 100), and prepare by making notes about what you will write, and then draft the whole document before typing or writing the final version as neatly as possible.

Write an application letter to accompany the CV – consult *The Help Section* first (page 101).

26. Research a holiday resort

Completed:

Write or telephone to a holiday resort for up-to-date information about facilities, accommodation, etc. Read about the resort and the area in which it is situated by using the library.

Write a short report about the resort, illustrating it with images, such as photographs and charts.

Based on your report, give a short (e.g. 10 minute) talk to your group, illustrated with some images, and use a simple feedback sheet (see *Obtain feedback* on page 96) to obtain an evaluation of your performance.

27. Design a questionnaire

Completed:

Design a questionnaire to investigate a specific, straightforward topic – perhaps agreed in advance with your tutor/assessor. The topic may be connected with your GNVQ (e.g. the holiday, eating or leisure preferences of a group of people) or may be about other issues. The people questioned may be your fellow learners, family and friends, or members of the public.

You may have to telephone one or more people to obtain permission to use the questionnaire (e.g. if you wish to go into private premises to question members of the public).

Be realistic about the length of the questionnaire – people may not be able to give you a lot of their time; and about the number of people you can question in the time that you have. Read about questionnaires in *The Help Section* (page 103) before drafting your questions. Test the questionnaire on two or three people before preparing the final version.

Once you have had the questionnaires returned to you completed, analyse the results, taking care to interpret them honestly and not to put your own bias on the results.

Write a short report that describes the topic you investigated and the results of the survey (include a copy of the questionnaire as an appendix). Bear in mind who the report is for. Use images, such as tables and charts, to illustrate the report.

Based on your report, give a short (e.g. 10 minute) talk to your group. Invite people from another group to attend. Illustrate your talk with some images. Leave time after your talk for a discussion of some of the issues raised. Use a simple feedback sheet (see *Obtain feedback* on page 96) to obtain an evaluation of your performance.

28. Investigate a facility

Completed:

Select a facility (e.g. sports centre, hotel, nursery, art gallery, etc.). Decide on a specific topic you wish to find out about (e.g. how food and drink are provided for visitors; what customer services are provided; access for disabled people; health and safety issues, etc.).

Use the telephone to arrange a visit during which you can talk to an appropriate member of staff about the topic you wish to investigate. Request some information in advance (e.g. leaflets) if it is easy to provide (you should offer to send a stamped addressed envelope).

Prepare for the visit by using a library to consult relevant books or articles on the topic (see *Using a library* on page 123). Draw up a checklist of questions you wish to ask.

Make the visit, and discuss your questions with a member of staff at the facility. Make adequate notes of the meeting or, if possible, tape the meeting, with the permission of the member of staff.

After the visit, read your notes or playback and make notes from the tape. Write a short report about the facility, illustrated with appropriate images.

Write a letter of thanks to staff you talked to at the facility. Enclose a copy of your report, if your tutor thinks it appropriate.

Based on your report, give a short (e.g. 10 minute) talk to your group. Invite people from the facility to attend. Illustrate your talk with some images. Leave time after your talk for a discussion of some of the issues raised, and use a simple feedback sheet (see *Obtain feedback* on page 96) to obtain an evaluation of your performance.

29. Observe a reception area

Completed:

Read the part of *The Help Section* about speaking and listening to people (pages 87–90). Use a library to read books and articles about the skills needed to organise and run a reception area (see *Using a library* on page 123).

Telephone an organisation or facility (e.g. hotel, sports centre, hospital) to request to spend some time (perhaps two half-days) observing the way the reception area works. Be specific about the sorts of things you wish to learn (e.g. record keeping, appropriate behaviour, telephone manner, etc.). You may have to put your request in writing. If so, write a letter to confirm your visit.

When you make your visit to the reception area, introduce yourself and explain what you hope to observe. Remember to dress and behave appropriately for a reception area. Observe, ask

appropriate questions, discuss issues with the staff and make notes of the things you learn.

After the visit, read your notes and write a short report that states where you went, what you observed, and comments on any features of the use of communication in the reception area that you found interesting. The report may be illustrated by appropriate images, including a diagram showing the layout of the reception area.

Write a letter of thanks, both to the reception staff and to the organisation. Enclose a copy of your report, if your tutor thinks it appropriate.

Based on your report, give a short (e.g. 10 minute) talk to your group. Invite people from the reception area to attend. Illustrate your talk with some images. Leave time after your talk for a discussion of some of the issues raised, and use a simple feedback sheet (see *Obtain feedback* on page 96) to obtain an evaluation of your performance.

30. Observe people speaking and listening

Completed:

Read the part of *The Help Section* about speaking and listening (pages 87–90) and make notes about the main features to look out for when observing people holding conversations. Draw up a checklist (you may want to concentrate on particular aspects of speaking and listening, such as eye contact, tone of voice, choice of vocabulary; or you may want to include many features).

Select particular situations and observe people speaking and listening. For example, you may observe adults speaking with children in a nursery; staff talking with elderly people in a residential centre; teenagers discussing an issue in a refectory. In some instances, you may have to obtain permission to observe, by telephoning and/or writing to discuss the project.

Make notes during the observation – possibly by recording a particular behaviour each time it occurs. If you can obtain permission to tape the situation, and the use of a video or tape recorder does not distort the conversation too much (i.e. people do not change their behaviour because they know they are being recorded) this may help you observe more closely.

After your observations are complete, review your notes (and tapes if you have them) and write a short report about what you have learned about the ways in which people speak and listen in particular situations. Take care to ensure the anonymity of people observed by referring to them as fictitious names or as letters (person A, person B, etc.). Illustrate the report with appropriate images (e.g. a table of results; a diagram of body language or layout of a room).

Based on your report, give a short (e.g. 10 minute) talk to your group, inviting people from other groups who may be interested. Illustrate your talk with some images. Leave time after your talk for a discussion of some of the issues raised. Use a simple feedback sheet (see *Obtain feedback* on page 96) to obtain an evaluation of your performance.

Combined assignments for level 3

Level: there is no reason why LEVEL 2 students should not complete these assignments. So long as all LEVEL 2 performance criteria are covered, they may produce evidence of achievement.

31. Investigate non-discriminatory practice

Completed:

Read the part of *The Help Section* about uses of language that avoid discrimination against disabled people, women, and members of ethnic minorities (page 93). Carry out some background research in a library to consider what effects discrimination may have on people's health and well-being, and their access to leisure and tourism facilities (including educational) and hospitality and catering outlets (see *Using a library* on page 123).

Investigate a small number of facilities and outlets in your locality (e.g. pubs, clubs, colleges, shops) to see what measures they take to avoid discrimination and encourage access. Try to focus your enquiry upon specific issues (e.g. use of mission statements; training of staff; wheelchair access, etc.).

Telephone to discuss and arrange a visit to your

selected facilities, sending a follow-up letter of confirmation if necessary.

Devise a simple questionnaire or checklist of questions to help you find out the information you seek. Remember that discrimination is a potentially sensitive subject to investigate. Be tactful and sensitive in your questioning.

Visit the facilities to talk to people and discuss the issues about non-discriminatory practices that you wish to focus on.

Write a report, illustrated with suitable images, that sets out your findings and that maintains the anonymity of the organisations and individuals who participated.

Write letters of thanks to the people who co-operated in the project. Enclose a copy of your report, if your tutor thinks it appropriate.

Based on your report, give a short talk to your group. Invite people from the facilities to attend. Illustrate your talk with some images. Leave time after your talk for a discussion of some of the issues raised, and use a simple feedback sheet (see *Obtain feedback* on page 96) to obtain an evaluation of your performance.

32. Investigate a healthy diet

Completed:

There are conflicting views about what constitutes a healthy diet. Do some background reading on the topic in a library. Make notes of the main points you discover (see *Using a library* on page 123).

Identify a group of people you can question about their views on diet (e.g. a mixed sample of people in a residential home for the elderly, staff in a nursery school, your own tutors, or shoppers in a local supermarket). Draw up a questionnaire or checklist of questions on the topic of a healthy diet and use it to find out people's views.

Write a report, illustrated with suitable images, that sets out your findings and that maintains the anonymity of the organisations and individuals who participated.

Based on your report, give a short talk to your group. Invite people from outside your school/college to take part. Illustrate your talk with some images.

Leave time after your talk for a discussion of some of the issues raised. Use a simple feedback sheet (see *Obtain feedback* on page 96) to obtain an evaluation of your performance.

33. Investigate team work

Completed:

Read the part of *The Help Section* about speaking and listening (page 87), especially those aspects, such as *Establishing and maintaining rapport* (page 88), that are particularly important to working in teams. Use a library to do some background reading and make notes on teams and team building (see *Using a library* on page 123).

Identify a few facilities or outlets (e.g. a hotel, a pub, a residential home, a school) in which you could investigate the issue of effective teamwork. Telephone them to discuss what you wish to do and to arrange access. It would be wise to send a letter confirming arrangements.

Based on your background reading, prepare a simple questionnaire or checklist of questions about effective teamwork. Visit the places with which you have made arrangements and talk to people there about their perceptions of teamwork.

Write a report, illustrated with suitable images, that sets out your findings and that maintains the anonymity of the organisations and individuals who participated.

Write letters of thanks to the people who co-operated in the project. Enclose a copy of your report, if your tutor thinks it appropriate.

Based on your report, give a short talk to your group. Invite people from the facilities to take part. Illustrate your talk with some images. Leave enough time after your talk for a discussion of some of the issues raised. Use a simple feedback sheet (see *Obtain feedback* on page 96) to obtain an evaluation of your performance.

34. Investigate the influence of external factors on an industry's performance

Completed:

All sectors of industry are affected by a range of external factors – government policy, economic performance, levels of world trade, wars, changes in people's expectations, etc. Choose the industry that you are interested in and investigate the factors that have affected it the over the past 5 years, and the factors that you think are likely to affect it in the next 5 years.

Carry out a library search, making use of trade publications, newspapers and journals, as well as books (see *Using a library* on page 123).

Telephone or write to a few key people in the industry in your locality (e.g. a catering manager, a health care administrator, a tourist facility operator) to arrange to interview them about their perceptions of external factors. Draw up a checklist of questions to ask them, based on your reading.

Write a report, illustrated with suitable images, that sets out your findings and that maintains the anonymity of the organisations and individuals who participated.

Write letters of thanks to the people who co-operated in the project. Enclose a copy of your report, if your tutor thinks it appropriate.

Based on your report, give a short talk to your group. Invite the people you interviewed to take part. Illustrate your talk with some images. Leave time after your talk for a discussion of some of the issues raised. Use a simple feedback sheet (see *Obtain feedback* on page 96) to obtain an evaluation of your performance.

35. Plan an event

Completed:

Working with others, plan an event (e.g. a sponsored walk to raise money for charity; a visit to a place of interest; a dance). Negotiate roles in the team to cover all aspects of planning for and organising the event, to include, for example:

- making telephone calls and writing letters to make preliminary arrangements, obtain permissions, find out information;
- ensuring adequate health and safety provision for the event;
- advertising and publicity.

Consider how effectively the planning team works

together. Keep a record of all team meetings, particularly of decisions made and who will carry them out. Make notes also of how the team operates. Who plays what role in the team? Do people really listen to one another and reach collective decisions? What, if any, are the aspects of communication that the team should try to improve?

Hold the event.

Carry out an evaluation of the event, against criteria agreed in advance by the team. The evaluation process may include feedback from participants at the event.

Keep a careful record of your own part in the planning, running and evaluation of the event and match this against the performance criteria for the Communication elements.

36. Investigate the layout of accommodation

Completed:

Telephone and/or write to negotiate access to one or more residential facilities (e.g. hotels, residential centres, halls of residence, etc.).

Visit the facilities and draw simple diagrams showing the layout of accommodation.

Evaluate the efficiency and suitability of the accommodation, taking account of the needs of potential users, including disabled people, children and the elderly.

Return to the facilities to discuss your evaluation with staff. This will require tact and careful research on your part. Prepare for your visit by drawing up a checklist of issues and questions.

Write a report, illustrated with suitable images, that sets out the results of your investigation and that maintains the anonymity of the organisations and individuals who participated.

Write letters of thanks to the people who co-operated in the project. Enclose a copy of your report, if your tutor thinks it appropriate.

Based on your report, give a short talk to your group. Invite people from the facilities you visited to take part. Illustrate your talk with some images. Leave time after your talk for a discussion of some of the issues raised. Use a simple feedback sheet (see *Obtain feedback* on page 96) to obtain an evaluation of your performance.

THE HELP SECTION

What is language?

Language is a constantly changing human attribute, and the English language is now spoken throughout the world by about a thousand million people.

Language is not only about communicating with others. Much of our thinking is carried out in language and we 'talk to ourselves' from time to time to clarify our thoughts.

However, the main purpose of language assessed as a core skill is communication: the use of language to express and understand information, opinions and instructions. Through language we interpret and understand the world, as well as transmit ideas about it.

Speaking and listening are natural human activities and most people cannot avoid becoming very skilful at an early age. Writing and reading, however, are skills that we have to learn and, like all skills, they can be improved by practice.

Images are used in writing and speaking to illustrate points, and sometimes – for example, if two architects are discussing ideas – may almost take the place of words.

All four elements of Communication are inter-related:

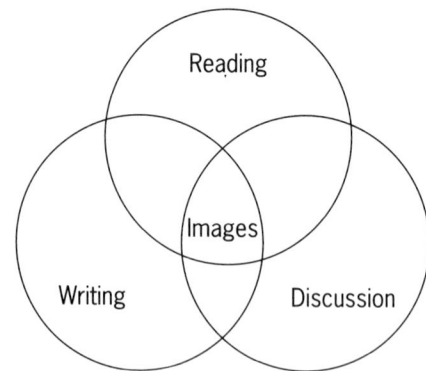

Failure to communicate effectively is the cause of much unhappiness and is estimated to cost billions of pounds a year due to stress-related illness causing absence from education and work. In a democratic society, it is essential that people express their views and respect those of others – people who cannot communicate effectively may become the victims of those who can.

Element 2.1 and 3.1: Take part in discussions

SPEAKING AND LISTENING

The ease or difficulty of speaking and listening depends mainly on three factors:

- what is being spoken about
- who you are speaking to
- whether you are speaking face to face or on the telephone

Even young children talk differently to a friend, a parent and a teacher. By the time people are in their teens, most have a wide repertoire of language styles to fit particular situations.

STOP AND THINK
Think about times when your own style of speaking may change (e.g. in an interview; making a presentation; talking to a baby; talking to a foreigner who speaks little English).

It is important that you use the appropriate style for the situation. For instance, it is not a good idea to shout at an interview; and it may not be appropriate to speak softly and slowly, choosing your words with care, at a football match.

Style is affected by a number of factors, including:

- The situation in which the language is being used – for example, are you making a formal presentation, or having an informal chat?

- The subject that is being communicated – is it complex (e.g. technical, scientific, sensitive) or straightforward?

- The audience for which you speak or write – how well do you know your listeners or readers? How much do they know about the subject?

The manner in which you speak refers to the fact that, 'It ain't what you say, it's the way that you say it'. Manner involves observing social conventions which are appropriate to the situation, and speaking in an appropriate tone of voice. Our tone changes according to different situations, and it is made up of a number of factors including:

- Pitch – we tend to talk with a higher or rising pitch when excited, talking to babies, or asking questions.

- Loudness – we tend to talk more loudly to people we suspect may not understand us.

- Speed – we tend to talk more quickly when we get excited, or feel nervous.

STOP AND THINK
Make a note of the different ways of speaking used by you, your friends and family. Under what circumstances do you alter the way you speak?

Grice's maxims

Paul Grice (1975) reasoned that conversation is based on a cooperative principle, built upon four maxims:

- *Quantity*: say neither too much nor too little. Be as informative as you need to be.

- *Quality*: say only what you believe you can show to be true.

- *Relevance*: keep to the topic.

- *Manner*: express yourself clearly and in an orderly way, avoiding jargon and ambiguity.

If a maxim is broken (e.g. if someone rambles on, lies, wanders from the point, or deliberately uses obscure words) there may be an attempt by the listener to 'mend fences' and assume there is a good reason for the speaker to talk in that way. If there is not a good reason, the speaker may come to be regarded as a bore or labelled a liar.

Sometimes people deliberately break a maxim for fun, or because the principle of cooperation comes first. If someone intends to borrow a pen and you answer their question, 'Do you have a pen?' with 'Yes, thanks', it may be that you are deliberately flouting maxim 3: Relevance. Jokes are often based on breaking the 'rules' of language. The art of storytelling deliberately breaks maxim 2: Quality, by sometimes inventing fabulous lies. Very honest people may lie or equivocate so as not to hurt people's feelings; the ugly-baby syndrome requires that we sometimes bend the truth so as not to hurt people. This is known as 'tact' – an intuitive understanding of the appropriate thing to do or say.

Underlying Grice's maxim is the rule that helps people to co-exist: be polite. Robin Lakoff (1977) suggested three rules for politeness:

1) Formality: neither impose nor remain aloof.

2) Hesitancy: give people spoken to room to express their own views; don't box people in.

3) Equality or Camaraderie: act as though you and the person you are talking to are equal. Make the other person feel good.

Underlying all these 'rules' are two even more fundamental ones: be yourself (self-respect) and be sincere (respect the other person).

The right to speak

Each person has a unique voice, which is why when an old friend telephones, even after years of separation, we recognise the person by the voice. Everyone has a right to speak, and we have a responsibility to listen to what other people have to say.

There is evidence that men – especially white, middle-class men with 'educated' South-East England accents – dominate in many speech situations. In doing so they may discourage others from speaking. Men in general have tended to speak, in public situations, more than women, whereas women have been more likely than men to express their thoughts and ideas with friends and colleagues.

A voice specialist, Patsy Rodenburg (*The Right to Speak*, 1992, Methuen) thinks that British society does not encourage people to express themselves freely. She recounted working at Eton where she was 'stunned by the open vocal release and freedom', compared to working in a comprehensive in a depressed area of London where, 'Discussion was minimal. It was rare...it was all just slightly short of vocal repression.'

 STOP AND THINK
Reflect on your own speaking and listening. Do you ever intimidate? Are you ever intimidated?

Reflect on your words

Cooperative social life is based upon being self-conscious or reflective about the effect our words and actions have upon other people. A dog can communicate by, for example, barking or wagging its tail, but these gestures are not self-conscious in the way that human communication can be. If I poke out my tongue to a friend she may laugh; if I poke it out to a stranger on a train he may take offence. A dog will bark at anyone if it is in a barking mood. Some human beings behave in this way too, saying or doing things without fully comprehending the effect on other people. In very young children this may be acceptable but as people grow they are expected to be more sensitive and aware of others.

Verbal bullying

The saying 'Sticks and stones will break your bones but words will never hurt you', is untrue. What people say – or fail to say – can hurt other people very deeply. It is possible to bully, sometimes in subtle ways by, for example, making disparaging or sarcastic remarks or by inappropriate responses (e.g. laughing, sneering, looking away) in order to 'put down' another person. Often bullies have themselves been bullied and show their fear and lack of self-respect by their behaviour. However, this does not diminish the hurtfulness of verbal bullying.

If you are being bullied, it is wise not to suffer in silence – be assertive, or talk it over with someone else.

Establishing and maintaining rapport

Rapport is about harmonious relationships between people. Sometimes you hit it off with another person straight away – there is a rapport between you, though it may be difficult to explain why. There are also people to whom you find it difficult to relate.

In working situations we have to get on with all sorts of people. It is important that, without being shallow or insincere, we try to smooth relationships, to establish as much rapport as we can, because by doing so everyone's life is more pleasant and work tasks are accomplished more easily.

One good way to establish and maintain rapport is to give people time, listen to them, talk to them. Often you will discover that you have some common ground after all (rapport is often established by talking about subjects that interest both people).

Finding common ground with another person is often about establishing what experiences and interests you share. This is the reason why the weather is often used as a conversation opener. When people are in love they often talk about themselves because the other person is fascinated by just about anything they say. Normally, however, we must try a little harder to find the common ground.

Working in teams

Both in employment and domestic life, it can greatly facilitate tasks and the well-being of individuals if people collaborate and act in teams, rather than behaving as isolated individuals. Much has been written about the roles people play in teams (e.g. leader, coordinator, clown, outsider, etc.) and the stages that teams may go through as they come together, carry out their task and then disintegrate (e.g. forming, storming, 'norming', performing and mourning). Underlying all successful teamwork is the ability of a number of people in the team to communicate effectively. There are no magic formulas about how to do this – no two teams are identical – but much of what is written in this help section about speaking and listening is of importance to individuals who wish to contribute to successful teamwork. It is also important to document team meetings accurately (see *Documenting a meeting*, p.101).

Listening skills

One of the most important skills for communicating well is the ability and the willingness to listen. Possessing ears does not automatically make people good listeners.

> ❗ **STOP AND THINK**
> Take it in turns with another person to talk about a subject that interests you (e.g. a holiday, a film). For the first two minutes the listener should pay attention, then they should 'switch off' for two minutes, and finally, should listen again. Swop roles and repeat the exercise.

The effect of listening behaviour is to help establish a feeling of harmony between people, even if they disagree about what is being said. It is inevitable that people will disagree about all sorts of subjects, but they can often do so in ways that enable them to find a basis for discussion and some common ground.

The effect of non-listening behaviour is to make the speaker feel a variety of negative emotions – wounded pride, humiliation, anger, resentment.

> **How can you tell if someone is listening or not?**

Listening behaviour	Non-listening behaviour
Eye contact – not all the time but enough to show attention and interest	Too little eye contact (e.g looking around the room, reading, staring into space)
Body posture – orientation towards the speaker	Physically turning away
Verbal cues – making encouraging sounds (e.g. 'Mhm, yes...I agree')	Saying little or nothing so that silence means inattention, or that you are just awaiting your turn to speak
Other cues – nodding in agreement, smiling encouragingly	Frowning, sneering, sniggering

> **How did the experience of not being listened to make you feel?**

None of these emotions helps to promote healthy relationships.

It is particularly difficult to listen when someone is criticising you – it is easy to ignore what is said because of feelings of wounded pride or anger. Try to concentrate on *what* is said and not on who says it, how it is said or your own feelings.

Talking down to people

If you listen to a mother talking to a young baby, she will often use a type of question that she does not expect an answer to, but that is intended to encourage communication in smiles and sounds. Questions, such as 'Are you going to give me a big smile, are you?' are often said in a higher pitch of voice than normal, and with rising intonation at the end. If a mother said, 'Who's a lovely baby, then?' and the baby replied, 'Search me. What about the one over there?' she would be astonished – and would move on to real questions, that require a reasoned reply. 'Babytalk', as it is called, is important in establishing a close bond between parent and child (lovers too, often use a similar type of language for the same reason).

When adults talk to very old people, or to people with disabilities, they may be tempted to use similar forms of 'babytalk', even when the older person is perfectly capable of reasoned conversation. Listen to

you're a sweet old feller, aren't you!

When adults talk to very old people they may be tempted to use 'Baby Talk'.

this conversation, in which the helper talks with higher pitch than normal, and with rising intonation at the end of sentences:

>Older person: I had a party.

>Helper: You used to have a big party?

>Older person: I don't feel old.

>Helper: Oh you don't feel old?

This is not a normal conversation. The helper is talking down to the older person.

 STOP AND THINK
What sort of reply to the older person's first statement, 'I had a party', might be given in a normal, adult to adult, conversation?

If the helper had responded to the first statement adult to adult, appropriate replies may have been: 'What kind of party?', 'I love parties.', or 'I thought you were the kind of person to enjoy a good party!'.

However, instead of responding, the helper merely repeats the older person's statement in a different form. And, to make matters worse, when the older person then says, 'I don't feel old', the helper repeats that too, instead of saying something like 'I'm sure you don't' or 'You don't look old'.

The best way to encourage other people to talk is to listen and to respond appropriately. That is what a parent is encouraging a baby to do when making 'babytalk'; that is what we should all try to do when talking to other people, adult to adult.

MAKING AND RECEIVING COMPLAINTS

Most complaints can be dealt with by simple courtesy from both sides. Whether making or receiving a complaint try to avoid types of attacking behaviour that are likely to lead to antagonism rather than to the resolution of the problem. Attacking behaviour may involve sarcasm, anger, belittling and other ways of focusing on the feelings of people, rather than on the problem itself.

Making a complaint

Before making a complaint check your facts (e.g. are you sure there is a fuse in the plug? Are you being reasonable?).

Human communication is based on a principle of cooperation (see *Grice's maxims*) so most people find making a complaint rather embarrassing, even when they have solid cause. If you think you have a reason to complain, be assertive (see *Speaking assertively*):

- Ensure that you are speaking to someone who can deal with the complaint.

- State the complaint clearly, without necessarily blaming anyone.

- State what you want done (be reasonable).

There are times when you may be quite justified in being angry, and showing it.

When making a complaint, try to be neither aggressive nor timid. Speak in a tone and manner suited to any other conversation with the person being spoken to. Remember the old saying, 'You catch more with honey than with vinegar'. Nevertheless, there are times when you may be quite

justified in becoming angry, and showing it. This should always be after you have tried other approaches, rather than as your initial reaction.

Receiving a complaint

The person receiving a complaint should listen attentively and, if necessary, check that they have understood what the complaint is about. Depending on the nature of the complaint, they should either investigate immediately or offer to do so as soon as possible.

Most workplaces have standard procedures (formal or understood) to deal with complaints that may include recording the complaint, and bringing it to a manager's attention if the complaint is serious, etc.

Most complaints can be effectively dealt with by listening and reacting straight away in a sensible manner, avoiding time-consuming form filling, and argument.

Speaking assertively

Assertive behaviour means behaving in a manner that recognises that both you, and the person you are speaking with, have rights and responsibilities. You both have a right to express your opinions, and this right comes with a responsibility to listen with attention and respect to what the other person has to say.

Assertive speaking and listening is neither aggressive (e.g. shouting, dominating, using sarcasm, not listening) nor timid (e.g. not daring to say what you feel, tolerating the other person's aggression).

Some of the characteristics of assertive speaking are:

- listening to the other person and being attentive to what they are saying;

- focusing on the matters being discussed, rather than on personal feelings (for example, saying 'I don't agree with that point', rather than 'I don't agree with you, you are pig headed');

- responding in a tone and manner suited to talking to a fellow human being (i.e. with respect – shown by appropriate pitch, loudness, speed, etc.);

- if appropriate, saying no to a request, without necessarily giving a reason;

- maintaining your opinions, and your right to hold them, without backing down or forcing them on the other person;

- changing your opinion, agreeing with the other person, if there are grounds for doing so;

- owning your opinions by saying 'I think', rather than, 'they say', 'people think', 'it's common sense' or 'everyone knows that...'.

AVOID BIAS AND DISCRIMINATION IN YOUR USE OF LANGUAGE

It is possible, even without knowing it, to offend other people by your use of language. Try to be sensitive to the feelings of other people. In particular, avoid stereotyping people by lumping them all together in big groups that are supposedly all alike (e.g. people with disabilities, women, ethnic groups). People are unique individuals. No two are alike, and like you, they are all susceptible to feeling patronised or insulted. Put yourself in the other person's shoes. How would the words you use strike you? Remember, it is not true that 'words will never hurt you'.

While trying to be aware of other people's feelings, don't go too far and use unhelpful terms such as, for example, 'visually challenged' when you mean 'partially sighted'.

Gender

For thousands of years, in many societies, women have been treated as subordinates to men. Their voices were not expected to be heard on important matters. Men did not take kindly to being contradicted by a woman, and women were not always listened to as attentively as men – men 'talked', women 'gossiped'. Some terms may be positive when applied to men but negative when applied to women (e.g. 'ambitious'). These days men and women are more aware of this systematic discrimination and are more prepared to watch out for the ways in which it may be perpetuated in language.

Whether speaking or writing, the word 'he' or 'his' is often used to mean an unspecified person of either

sex. This can have the effect of excluding women (e.g. 'When an old friend telephones we recognise him by his voice', may not produce an image of a woman as well as a man). Sometimes the problem can be avoided by using a different sentence structure (e.g. 'When an old friend telephones we recognise who it is by their voice); sometimes by using she *and* he, although this is rather clumsy (e.g. 'When an old friend telephones we recognise him or her by his or her voice'). If you cannot avoid a gender-specific pronoun use 'he' if you are male, and 'she' if you are female.

Nearly half the people in employment are women and they have all sorts of jobs, but there are still many gender-stereotyped words used (e.g. 'foreman' rather than 'supervisor'; 'air hostess' rather than 'cabin staff'; 'chairman' rather than 'chair').

Avoid using belittling terms such as 'bimbo', 'toy boy', 'hen-pecked', 'girls' to refer to grown people.

Use similar terms of address for men and women. Call everyone by their first names or their surnames; if you don't know the name of a person you are writing to, or can't use a general term(e.g. 'Dear Colleague', 'Dear Customer') then use 'Dear Sir/Madam'. Women may prefer to be addressed as Ms rather than Mrs or Miss (Mr does not show marital status).

Ethnic groups

Everyone belongs to an ethnic group that shares similar characteristics of geography, history, culture, religion, and so on. In Britain there are many ethnic groups (e.g. White, Afro-Caribbean, Asian). The groups can be sub-divided (e.g. White: English, Scottish, Welsh, Irish). Even these can be further divided (e.g. English: Londoners, Cornish, Liverpudlians). As you break down the groups you realise that the terms are just very simplified ways of grouping people who, as individuals, are very different. There is no such person as a typical Londoner, let alone a typical White, Afro-Caribbean or Asian.

So, avoid using language that lumps many people together and ignores their individual humanity. If you wish to refer to a group of people then try to be as precise as possible. Don't use 'English' or 'England' when you mean 'British' or 'Britain'. When referring to minority ethnic groups, avoid

using 'Black' when you mean 'Afro-Caribbean' or 'Asian'.

Try to avoid the use of 'black' in derogatory contexts (e.g. 'black marks', 'black spot', 'black sheep'). However, it is acceptable to use black as a normal adjective (e.g. 'blackboard').

Disability

One person in seven in Britain has a disability. That's over 6 million people, and you cannot lump together that number of people as one homogeneous mass. Once again, try to treat people as individuals or, when referring to a group, try to be as precise as possible (e.g. use 'partially deaf' or 'profoundly deaf' as appropriate, rather than just 'deaf', and 'blind' or 'partially sighted' as appropriate).

Avoid inaccurate and insulting terms (e.g. use 'people with Down's Syndrome', not 'Mongols'; 'people with Cerebral Palsy', not 'Spastics').

People with disabilities are no braver or more 'pathetic' than anyone else. They succeed because of their abilities, not because they are necessarily courageous. They are entitled to access to public facilities and other features of everyday life, such as employment and housing, without being patronised. They should not be talked down to, because most are capable of holding their own in any conversation.

Age

Older people, too, can be lumped together by insulting terms such as 'old dear' or 'old fogey', when most of them are perfectly fit and able. Most human characteristics are not age related – you can be a 'fogey' (behind the times) at any age.

Sexual orientation

The term 'homosexual', first used in 1869, has been the standard term to refer to people who are physically attracted to their own sex. The term has so often been used as one of abuse or discrimination that people who are homosexual have promoted the term 'gay'. 'Lesbian' is an acceptable term to refer to homosexual women.

Avoid terms that have often been used in a

demeaning way, such as 'queer', 'dyke', although some homosexual people may use these terms themselves.

Use the term 'partner', rather than 'spouse', because some people live together without being married. Some married people also prefer 'partner', rather than 'husband' or 'wife', although most married people probably find 'husband' and 'wife' perfectly acceptable.

STOP AND THINK
Are there any occasions when you show bias or discrimination against other people in the language you use?

THE SOUNDS OF ENGLISH

There are two main types of syllables: vowels and consonants. The English vowels are a, e, i, o, u. Any letters of the alphabet that are not vowels are examples of consonants. A consonant is a speech sound in which the breath is partly obstructed (e.g. by the tongue).

Accents

People are often self-conscious about the way that they speak, believing for example that they talk with the 'wrong' accent for the setting.

Everyone has an accent. Received Pronunciation (sometimes called 'Oxbridge' or 'BBC') is only one accent among many in English, and as a form of language it is neither better nor worse than any other accent. There is nothing wrong with an accent, as long as your communicating with other people is not hampered.

Be proud of your accent, but, if you think you have a problem with communication, or if you are self-conscious, you may do one or more of the following:

- Talk about accents with your family or friends. It is not a taboo subject: most people have thought about their accent at some time.

- Don't rush to change your accent – it is painful to hear someone trying too hard to talk in a way that is unnatural for them. Let your needs gradually change your accent over time.

- When you are nervous you tend to talk more quickly, and so emphasise your accent. So slow down. Talk at a pace at which you could sing the words.

Dialects

Groups of people sometimes use particular words or dialects to communicate with other members of the same group. A person from Yorkshire may call a total stranger 'love'; in Scotland a child may be called 'bairn'; and in Liverpool someone may say 'gissa' instead of 'give me'. The stronger the sense of group identity, the more likely it is that a particular dialect will be used. There are thousands of English dialects. They are associated with many factors, including:

- geographical area (e.g. Tyneside, Scotland)

- ethnic groups (e.g. Afro-Caribbean, South Asian)

- occupational groups (e.g. doctors, plumbers)

- youth culture (e.g. to describe clothes, music)

Some dialects change rapidly as they respond to constant shifts in people's ways of life. Sometimes, dialect expressions become part of standard English. For example, the Afro-Caribbean use of double negatives (e.g. 'There ain't no way'; 'Can't get no satisfaction') has become very widespread, partly through its use in music lyrics.

There is nothing wrong with using dialect in speech, as long as you can be understood clearly by your listeners. If you cannot be understood, it is not because your dialect is 'wrong' or because there is anything deficient with the understanding of the other person. It is usually simply that it can be difficult to tune-in to an unfamiliar dialect. It is up to you, as the speaker, to be aware of this.

For this reason it is important on occasions to be able to switch from dialect to a more standard English so that you can be understood in any circumstances you choose. This may be especially important when attending job interviews, where it is often expected that people will speak in ways that can be understood by other staff and any member of the public.

STOP AND THINK
If you think you have a problem with your dialect then follow the advice given in *Accents*.

NON-VERBAL COMMUNICATION

When we speak and listen we do not use only words, we also use a range of other means to communicate,

It is easy to jump to false conclusions about the meaning of a person's non-verbal communication.

such as sounds (e.g. 'mmm', 'oh', sighs), facial expressions, eye contact, body language, and the physical space we put between ourselves and others. It is extremely difficult to codify the huge number of variations of non-verbal language that arise in our interaction with other people. Be aware that it is easy to jump to false conclusions about the meaning of a person's non-verbal language. When we know someone well we can pick up subtle clues about their feelings from their non-verbal behaviour; with people we do not know well, especially if they are from a different cultural background, it can be difficult to 'read' their non-verbal behaviour accurately. If you want to find out more about this subject, carry out a library search.

USING THE TELEPHONE

When using the telephone we can't 'read' people's reactions in their eyes, posture and expressions. As a result we sometimes feel nervous. For this reason it is a good idea to gather your thoughts if you can before speaking.

Make notes if you are going to make an important telephone call (see *Making notes*). Try to relax. If you feel nervous you may talk too quickly (Let's get this over with) and talk incessantly (There mustn't be a moment's silence). Try to speak in a normal conversational tone, at a speed at which you could sing the words. Let the other person get a word in. Remember to say goodbye.

Answering a telephone call

Answering a telephone call can be almost as difficult as making a call. Remember to greet the caller appropriately: 'Hello', 'Good morning'. Give your own name or that of your organisation. Remember that tone of voice is particularly important when using the telephone. Try to sound relaxed, even if you are feeling tense. Speak at a normal speed and volume – try not to raise your voice or talk too quickly.

Make notes of any matters you wish to recall, especially if you need to pass a message to another person.

P: Prepare:
have any necessary facts or information to hand;
make sure you know who you wish to speak with;
have pen and paper handy to make notes.

H: Hello:
introduce yourself and your organisation;
ensure that you are speaking to an appropriate person.

O: Obvious:
speak clearly;
make the purpose of your call **obvious**;
listen carefully;
if necessary, ask questions to **clarify** what the other person is saying.

N: Note:
make a careful and accurate note of anything important, particularly names and numbers – read these back to the other person to check their accuracy.

E: End:
end the call politely, and thank the other person for their help.

Using an answerphone

Talking to a machine can be intimidating. Not only must you use the telephone, but you then have to relate to a disembodied voice. Don't be put off. Speak slowly after the tone, spelling any difficult words. Leave the following information: your name, the date and time of calling, what you are calling about, and a contact number. When leaving a number it helps to phrase it a few digits at a time so that the listener can write it down.

SPEAKING IN FORMAL SITUATIONS

When attending formal meetings (e.g. committees, interviews) or when making presentations, it is often helpful to prepare in advance.

Making notes

Many confident and experienced speakers prefer to have a few notes to help them talk on a topic, written clearly on index cards or sheets of paper. As you grow in confidence you may be able to speak 'off the cuff'. However, if you are unused to speaking to a group it is advisable to prepare notes and to follow them quite closely (see the section on *Making notes* on page 126). However, **do not just read straight from your notes – it will always sound stilted.**

Taking turns in meetings

It is often an unspoken rule that people will take turns to speak and to listen. It can be regarded as bad manners either to dominate discussion or to make too little effort to contribute.

It is a good idea to try to let everyone say something early in a meeting. The longer people stay silent, the more likely it is that they will say nothing for the whole meeting. There is some evidence that men tend to be more dominant than women in meetings – giving their views more often, and asking more questions – and that women listen more.

Encouraging people to contribute in meetings

It is important to ensure that everyone speaks who wishes to, and that no one dominates the discussion to the detriment of its purposes. A skilled chairperson in a formal meeting, and anyone skilled enough in an informal meeting, can help to encourage people to contribute by:

- knowing their names

- inviting people to introduce themselves

- inviting people by name to give their opinion

- thanking people for their contributions

And they can tactfully close down dominant people by thanking them for their contribution and inviting someone else to join in (e.g. 'Thanks for that. Would anyone else like to comment?').

Speaking to groups of people

It is helpful to try to find out in advance how much your audience will already know so that you do not bore them or talk above their heads. You should also bear in mind that people cannot concentrate on even the most fascinating speaker or topic for more than about 10 minutes before their minds begin to wander. As the saying goes, 'If you haven't struck oil in 10 minutes, stop boring'! Therefore:

- be selective about what you will say – don't try to make more than 4 or 5 different points;

- use some visual images (e.g. photographs, cartoons, or, if there are only a few people in your audience, objects to hand round) to keep the level of interest high.

Speaking to a group of people can be nerve-racking. Prepare adequately, but avoid over-preparation (it may make your speaking lack spontaneity); try to feel confident about your appearance, perhaps take a little more care about the way you dress; take a few deep breaths (e.g. 7-1-7 breathing: breathe in to a count of 7, hold your breath for 1, breathe out for 7).

When making a presentation, especially if there are many people present, it can be difficult to judge whether you are establishing rapport. A more conscious effort may be needed to decide whether people are listening attentively or have 'switched off'.

The judicious (i.e. timely and appropriate) use of humour may help to enliven a presentation and keep the audience alert.

Some speakers like to begin with a humorous remark to gain the audience's attention, then use a little humour every few minutes to retain the audience's interest, and end with something humorous to leave the audience with positive feelings. However, if this is done in a mechanical way, or if humour is not appropriate, this can have a negative effect.

Obtain feedback

After a talk or presentation, it can be useful to ask the audience for feedback by, for example, completing an evaluation sheet like this:

Please comment on the following aspects of the presentation (please circle your responses):

How much did you know about the subject before the talk?

A lot   Quite a lot   Not much   Nothing

How well do you know the speaker?

Very well   Quite well   A little   Not at all

Organisation of ideas (evidence of background reading; logical structure, etc.)

Excellent   Good   Fair   Poor

Clarity of expression (choice of words, tone of voice, etc.)

Excellent   Good   Fair   Poor

Use of images (appropriate images, used at appropriate time, etc.)

Excellent   Good   Fair   Poor

Other Comments (e.g. mannerisms, length of talk, etc.):

Thank you for your comments

This feedback sheet provides information about the success of the talk and the nature of the audience – both of which are useful when gathering evidence of achievement.

Interviews

Interviews are potentially stressful situations. Whether you are being interviewed, or interviewing someone it is important to follow the advice in the previous sections, particularly about preparing by making some notes, speaking in an appropriate manner, establishing rapport, listening, being assertive, and avoiding bias and discrimination.

It is particularly important to make people feel comfortable and to ensure that the purpose of the interview is clear.

For the interviewer, it is also important to use open questions that give the person being interviewed plenty of scope to express their views. Open questions often begin with words such as 'How', 'What', and 'Why'. They invite the speaker to expand on what they have to say. For example, the question 'How would you like your career to develop?' gives more scope to reply than 'Would you like to gain promotion?' Similarly, 'What are your favourite pastimes?' is a better, more open question than 'Do you like swimming?'

The person interviewing may also summarise at various points in order to keep the conversation focused, and to make sure that the person being interviewed is being understood. This is especially important during assessment, counselling or appraisal interviews which serve the purpose of allowing the interviewee to express their thoughts and feelings. A typical summarising statement may begin: 'Let me make sure that I have understood you...'; and may end by a statement such as 'Is that a fair summary?', or 'Do you wish to add anything to that?'

Relaxing the voice

In situations where you feel your voice becoming constricted, try to relax your jaw, shoulders, chest and abdomen. Take a few deep breaths. Breathe in, speak out. Take your time. Breathe in, speak out. And remember to listen.

RECORDING THE VOICE

You may need to record yourself or others in discussions, in order to present evidence for assessment.

Tape recorders often distort the voice, making it sound less vibrant than we expect. You may find that you do not like your own voice on tape. To get the best out of an audio or video recording, use a free-standing microphone and experiment with distance and sound levels until you get a clear recording. This process need take only a minute or so but will improve the sound quality, especially if you wish to submit a recording as evidence of achievement.

Element 2.2 and 3.2: Produce written material

WRITING

Writing is a highly complex activity, at which most people become proficient. It is not just written down speech. Even the dialogue of a stage play or a TV soap opera is only an approximation to everyday speech, with its pauses, hesitations and emphases.

Just as each person's speech is unique, so no two people write exactly alike. Writing is an expression of individuality, as well as an attempt to communicate with other people.

Transactional writing often has strong elements of persuasion.

Types of writing

Most professional, everyday writing is *transactional* (i.e. it uses language that is intended to inform or influence other people), and it is this aspect of language that is developed and assessed as a core skill in Communication.

Transactional language can, for the sake of clarity, be sub-divided by purpose into:

Informative = desire to make information available through, e.g. writing records, reports, letters. The information should be true, relevant, reliable and clearly stated.

Instructive/persuasive = desire to influence the reader, either through regulation, if the roles of writer and reader carry with them the authority to regulate, and compliance is assumed (e.g. instructions, requests expressed in memos); or through persuasion if the audience is more distant and less controlled by the writer (e.g. advertising, advising, recommending in reports or letters).

Most transactional writing falls into the informative category, but it often has strong elements of persuasion, either directly through what is stated, or indirectly through the words chosen, the layout of the document, etc.

You should be able to write for a variety of purposes, including to give information, to get information, to express or obtain opinions, to exchange ideas and to present an argument.

Audience

When we speak face to face with other people we get rapid feedback because we can see and hear the audience react (even silence is a reaction – and a powerful one). When we write, however, the audience is more distant. For many professional documents the audience may even be people in general (e.g. potential customers). Writing rarely receives immediate feedback, and sometimes feedback is only obtained in a roundabout way (e.g. through sales figures). Because of this lack of immediate feedback when writing, it is important to think of the audience in a more conscious way than we usually do when speaking.

What *role* are you playing as a writer (e.g. expert, friend, adviser)? What role do you expect the

audience to play (e.g. general public, informed expert, friend)? The subject matter of any writing will be expressed differently depending on these roles. For example, many scientific documents are written by experts for experts, and may use complex terms that make the document impossible for non-experts to understand. In contrast, advertisements and many newspaper articles are written so that most people can understand them.

One way to build a sense of audience into your writing is to ask yourself two main questions:

> How well do you know the people for whom you are writing, and how well do they know you?

> How much do you think they will already know about the subject?

You should be able to communicate effectively in writing with a wide variety of people, including people who know you and the subject, and people who neither know you nor about the subject. It is necessary, therefore, to structure what you write to suit the audience.

Planning to write

Remember the three Ws:

> *Why* write (e.g. to inform, persuade, complain)?

> *Who* will read it (e.g. friend, colleague, public)?

> *What* format should it take (e.g. letter, report, memo)?

The process of thinking through these questions will also determine the general tone of your writing (e.g. formal, with your own personality concealed, or informal, with your own personality prominent).

It is important to keep your writing *focused* on the nature of the audience and the purpose of the writing. In this way you will be helped to meet the Performance Criteria for PRODUCE WRITTEN MATERIAL.

FORMATS OF WRITING

Different types of written document have conventional formats. Business letters are usually set out in a standard way; formal reports may follow a standard pattern set by an organisation. There is an underlying structure to most formats. It is usual to

make clear the subject or purpose of writing towards the beginning; to deal with important points before trivial ones; and to leave conclusions and recommendations until towards the end. This may seem obvious, but inexperienced writers sometimes take a long time to focus and to make plain to the reader what the subject is.

Remember that working people are often very busy. They want documents that are as brief as possible, but that deal clearly with the subject.

Memos

A memo (short for 'memorandum') is an informal note or letter that sets out information as briefly as possible. For convenience, memo outlines are often pre-printed. Here is a typical memo:

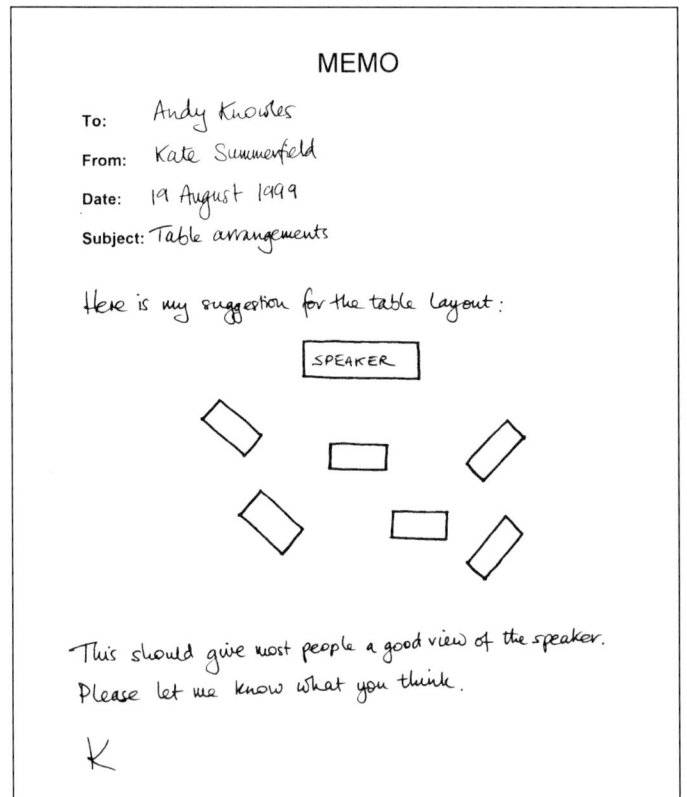

Letters

Letters serve all the possible purposes of written communication and often convey something of the personality of the writer, as well as information about the subject. It is often necessary to choose words with

care because *how* a subject is expressed is sometimes as important as *what* is expressed.

Here is a letter of complaint:

```
                                    14 Elm Dr.
                                    Elmchurch
                                    EX4 1RK
24 February 1997

The Planning Officer
District Council Offices
7 Lower George Street
Dissbury EX9 2JB

Dear Sir/ Madam,

I am writing to object to the proposed
building of a road across Green Belt land,
between Elmchurch and Brithely. My objections
are as follows:

Firstly, I object to even more Green Belt
land being lost to tarmac.

Secondly, I do not think that the road is
needed. Traffic in the area is heavy, but the
present road system is adequate.

Thirdly, I think that the environmental and
noise pollution of a new road, so close to
peaceful villages, would seriously affect the
health and well-being of local people. I am
especially worried about the possible harmful
effects on the health of our children.

Finally, I think that the huge sum of money
that the road would cost would be better
spent on providing better public transport,
health, education and housing — in other
words, on things that will improve the quality
of people's lives, instead of blighting them.

Yours faithfully,

Sandra Townsend

Sandra Townsend
```

STOP AND THINK
How effective do you think this letter is? Is the content relevant? Is it well structured? Is it written in an appropriate style? What does it tell you about the personality of the writer?

Letter writing conventions

People sometimes insist that 'Yours sincerely' goes with the use of a person's name, like 'Dear Mr Napier', whereas 'Yours faithfully' should go after the use of 'Dear Sir' or 'Dear Madam'. These are

trivial issues compared to getting the structure of a letter right – e.g. stating clearly in the opening paragraph what the letter is about, using an appropriate tone, and so forth. However, the standard conventions are:

- use a person's name ('Dear Mr Napier') when you know it, and close with 'Yours sincerely';

- use a person's first name ('Dear David') when you know the person quite well, or when writing to a colleague. You may then close with a variety of forms, such as 'Best wishes', instead of, or in addition to 'Yours sincerely';

- if you don't know someone's name but do know their sex, write 'Dear Sir' or 'Dear Madam', and close with 'Yours faithfully';

- if you don't know the sex of the person you are writing to, use an appropriate general term (e.g. 'Dear Customer') and if that is not possible use the rather clumsy 'Dear Sir/Madam';

The best way to familiarise yourself with the conventions of the layout of letters is to look at a few examples from companies and individuals.

Dates

The date is now most often written like this: 14 January 1998, without punctuation or 'th' after the 14. It may be placed below the sender's address, or above the address of the person to whom the letter is being sent.

Changing fashions in punctuating addresses

Taking the example of the address written at the top of a letter or on an envelope, you will find that fashions change in punctuation, and that what would once have been seen as incorrect may in time be regarded as perfectly acceptable:

Miss. G. Smith,	Ms G Smith
'The Larks',	The Larks
47, Cress Rd.,	47 Cress Road
Townley,	Townley
Yorks'.	Yorks YK1 5TN
YK1 5TN	

These changes have come about partly because of the cost of typing all the punctuation which, over a long period, can be very high for a large company (in terms of keying time). However, the changes are also the result of the more relaxed view that, as long

As long as what is written is clearly understandable, it is preferable to aim for simplicity.

as what is written is clearly understandable, it is preferable to aim for simplicity.

 STOP AND THINK
What conventions do you use to punctuate addresses and dates? Are you consistent?

Reports

Reports may be set out in any way that makes the contents of the document clear to the reader (PC3). It is often appropriate to use sub-headings, and sometimes to indicate sections with numbers or letters.

Very formal reports may be set out using the following sub-headings:

- *Terms of reference*, which state the subject of the report, and whether it includes recommendations. The terms of reference are normally set by whoever commissions the report;

- *The findings*, set out using appropriate sub-headings, numbering and/or lettering;

- *Conclusions*, which summarise the main points of the report;

- *Recommendations*, which may be listed in order of importance.

Most reports follow a less formal structure. The important thing is that the format suits the subject and presents information as clearly as possible. Remember that some information may be shown most clearly by using appropriate images.

Curriculum Vitae (CV)

A Curriculum Vitae or CV (literally, a run through your life) is often requested by employers when inviting applications for a job. It may also be sent out, with an accompanying letter, when enquiring if work is available. It is wise to type a CV.

Most people who read CVs are very busy and they wish to see at a glance whether you may be suited to a particular job. They do not wish to learn everything about your life's history – fascinating as that may be.

There is no right or wrong way to set out a CV, but remember that the visual impact it has may be an important factor in getting an interview. Here is a typical CV:

CURRICULUM VITAE

Paula Davis
37 Knight's Road,
Solihull,
West Midlands,
BM19 9RJ

tel: 0487 366782

AGE: 22

QUALIFICATIONS

St. Thomas More School
GCSEs: English   B
              Maths   C
              Physics   C
              History   A
              French   C

Soulbury College of Further Education
GNVQ
Advanced: Engineering   MERIT

EXPERIENCE

Technician, Brunel Engineering Ltd
At Brunel I am a design technician, working as a member of a small team. I have been abroad several times on projects.

INTERESTS
Dancing, travel, sports

Paula could have added more information, such as the dates of her qualifications and of her employment at Brunel Engineering; brief details of any significant work experience when a student; and the names and addresses of referees.

A typical CV is likely to contain the following order of information:

Name
Address
Telephone number
Age or date of birth
Education, with dates and results
Experience, with dates
Interests
Referees – usually two, with their names, addresses, telephone numbers and, if appropriate, positions.

STOP AND THINK
Should you experiment with different layouts of your CV and check their impact on friends and tutors?

Information should concentrate on what a prospective employer will need to know; and should emphasise positive achievements.

The accompanying letter

A CV is normally sent with an accompanying letter – typed or handwritten neatly – which should state clearly the job for which you are applying. You may also give brief details of why you are applying and what you are doing at present. The letter should end politely. Here is Paula's letter:

> 37 Knight's Road,
> Solihull,
> West Midlands,
> BM19 9RJ
>
> 14 January, 1998
>
> The Personnel Officer,
> Highbridge Engineering,
> Western Industrial Estate,
> Solihull,
> West Midlands,
> BM6 7QR
>
> Dear Mr Napier,
>
> Senior Design Technician, Ref: AN/471
>
> Thank you for sending me details of this post, for which I now wish to apply. As you will see from the enclosed CV, I am a qualified design technician, with several years experience of design projects with Brunel Engineering.
>
> I am happy at Brunel, but would like to gain experience in another firm and at a more senior level. I think that I am ready to take on more responsibility.
>
> I am available for interview at any time and look forward to hearing from you.
>
> Yours sincerely,
>
> *Paula Davis*
>
> Paula Davis
> Enc. CV

The letter could have been set out differently. For example, the addresses may have been written without punctuation; the paragraphs could have been indented, rather than blocked to the left-hand margin; as could the complimentary close, 'Yours sincerely'. However, these things are not that important. It is important that the letter includes all necessary information (PC1); is legible (PC2); is written following standard conventions of spelling, punctuation and grammar (PC2); and has an appropriate layout (PC3).

Documenting a meeting

Most organisations, whether public or private, hold a variety of meetings that need to be documented, so that people are given notice of what will be discussed; and a record of decisions taken. Company minutes, once they have been agreed and signed as a true record, may be used as legal evidence.

Company Annual General Meetings

A typical notice and agenda for a company Annual General Meeting looks like this:

> **NOTICE OF MEETING**
> Notice is given that the eighth Annual General Meeting of Hudson public limited company will be held at the Roxborough Hotel, Georgetown on Wednesday, 8 June at 11.00 a.m. for the transaction of the following business:
>
> **Ordinary business**
>
> *Resolution 1*
> THAT the accounts and reports of the directors and the auditors for the year ended 31 March 1998 be received.
>
> *Resolution 2*
> THAT the final dividend of 14 pence per share recommended by the directors be declared payable on 16 September 1998 to holders of ordinary shares registered at the close of business on 8 August 1998.
>
> *Resolution 3*
> THAT Mrs R J Hamilton be re-elected as a director of the company.

... and so the notice will continue, sometimes for pages, with accompanying documents, explanatory notes, and forms. Some notices may include agenda items.

However, most meetings are less formal than this, and are likely to follow this sequence:

Calling a meeting

A straightforward notice should be sent well in advance to everyone who may attend. The notice should include all necessary information (PC1); be legible (PC2); be written in conventional English (PC2); and be set out clearly (PC3). Here is a typical notice for a relatively informal meeting:

> **SWANFIELD COLLEGE**
> The next meeting of the Curriculum Development Committee will take place on Thursday, 16 June at 4.15 p.m. in the Green Room. Please submit items for the agenda, in writing, by Monday 6 June.

Once people have submitted agenda items these will be arranged by the Chair and/or the Secretary of the committee, like this:

> **SWANFIELD COLLEGE**
> The next meeting of the Curriculum Development Committee will take place on Thursday, 16 June at 4.15 p.m.in the Green Room.
>
> AGENDA
> 1) Apologies for absence
> 2) Minutes of the last meeting
> 3) Matters arising
> 4) Items for approval:
>   i   Electronic engineering course
>   ii Short courses on financial management
>   iii Module on development economics
> 5) Items for debate:
>   i   Staff development budget
>   ii Proposed amendments to assessment system
> 6) Any other business
> 7) Date of next meeting

This is a typical agenda structure for meetings in businesses, schools, colleges and government departments. It deals logically with the business of the meeting:

- Who is present/absent

- Agreement that the record of the last meeting is accurate

- An opportunity to report on any action taken as a result of the last meeting

- A list of the issues to be dealt with, in a particular order

- The opportunity to discuss other issues that people wish to raise

- The arrangements for the next meeting

Under *Matters arising* it is usual to concentrate on finding out if people have carried out what they were asked to do at the last meeting. It is not usual to re-open debates at length.

Under *Any other business* it is not usual to deal with important issues. These should be put on the agenda or tabled for the next meeting. If they are very pressing, however, they may be dealt with immediately, or a special or 'extraordinary' meeting may be called as soon as possible.

Beware agenda manipulation. The person drawing up an agenda can sometimes decide the items for debate. Items left out of an agenda may be more important than those included; and if important items are listed late in an agenda they may be ignored for lack of time.

The minutes

After the meeting, minutes will be drawn up, usually by a committee secretary, but often by a volunteer, or even the Chair. The minutes may look like this:

> **SWANFIELD COLLEGE**
> Minutes of the Curriculum Development Committee held on Thursday, 16 June.
> Present: [the names of everyone at the meeting]
>
> 1) Apologies for absence: [the names of those who could not attend and who sent their apologies]
> 2) Minutes of the last meeting: the minutes of the last meeting were accepted as a true record.
> 3) Matters arising: Matthew Archer reported that he had booked a speaker to talk about GNVQ at level 5.
> 4) Items for approval:
>   i   Electronic engineering course: approved.
>   ii Short courses on financial management: approved, subject to meeting an enrolment target of 15 people per course.
>   iii Module on development economics: approved.

```
5)  Items for debate:
    i    Staff development budget: it was
    agreed that two and a half per cent
    of budget will normally be given to
    staff development activities. Budget
    holders must ensure that they follow
    this norm and account for spending
    at the end of each financial year.
    ii   Proposed amendments to
    assessment system: it was agreed to
    set up a feasibility study, chaired
    by Dr Fraser, to consider the
    advantages of increased
    computerisation of assessment in the
    college. The study is to be
    submitted to the Committee by
    December.
6)  Any other business: a grant of £200
    was agreed to Ms Taylor towards
    conference expenses.
7)  Date of next meeting: the next
    meeting of the Curriculum
    Development Committee will take
    place on Thursday, 21 September at
    4.45 p.m. in the Oval Room.
```

This is a typical set of minutes from a meeting. Minutes should be as brief as possible, while being accurate and representing fairly what has been discussed. It is particularly important that, if action is to be taken, it is clear what this will be and who will carry it out (e.g. in the next meeting, under *Matters arising*, it will be checked that the task assigned to Dr Fraser has been carried out).

Questionnaire design

If you wish to gather the views of a large number of people, it may be necessary to write a questionnaire. (For a small sample of people, it is often preferable to interview them, using a checklist of questions. This usually yields more detailed information.)

Questionnaire design requires a lot of thought. Questions should be short and straightforward to avoid misinterpretation. To make the results of a questionnaire easier to analyse, it is best to use *closed* questions (i.e. giving respondents a limited range of answers to choose from). However, they do need to allow respondents to express their views accurately, which is not always the case with simple Yes/No choices.

Consider the following question:

Did you enjoy sports at school? Yes/No

The suggested response of Yes/No does not give the respondent an opportunity to express in-between feelings (e.g. they quite enjoyed swimming, hated cricket but loved soccer). You could supply a range of answers:

In general, how much did you enjoy sports at school? Very much/a lot/quite a lot/not at all

If you wanted to help people complete the questionnaire quickly, or if you wanted to focus on particular sports, you could give respondents alternatives to choose from, such as:

Please tick the sports you enjoyed at school:

☐ Athletics

☐ Badminton

☐ Basketball

etc.

Another way to gauge a person's opinion or experience more accurately than simply asking for a Yes/No response is to use a scale of letters or numbers, like this:

Please circle the response that most accurately represents your experience: 5 indicates very frequently, 1 indicates never.

I suffer from headaches   1   2   3   4   5

or

I go to the cinema   1   2   3   4   5

People are often very busy and therefore unable to give a lot of time to answering questionnaires.

You can also obtain an approximation of people's views by giving a few possible responses to a statement. For example:

> Please circle the response that is closest to your opinion.

> There is too much road traffic in Britain. Agree/ Neutral/ Disagree

However, for some questions you do need a Yes/No response, for example:

> Have you ever visited the United States? Yes/No

You may want to give people the option to expand, in which case questions should be *open*, leaving space for respondents to write what they want, for example:

> Which sports did you enjoy at school?

Another way to make a questionnaire more open is to ask 'Any Other Comments?'

People are often very busy and therefore unable to give a lot of time to completing questionnaires. Keep them as short as possible.

It is wise to trial or pilot a questionnaire before using it, to discover if any of the questions are difficult to understand or ambiguous; to test general reaction to the length and content of the questionnaire; and to assess how easy it is to interpret and record people's answers.

Don't forget to thank people for completing the questionnaire, either on the form itself or personally.

The assignment report

A report, written as part of a GNVQ assignment tends to follow a pattern:

- An introductory paragraph states the subject.

- A series of paragraphs, each of which develops the argument or line of reasoning.

Often the main topic of each paragraph will be stated in the opening sentence.

- The argument is supported by evidence (e.g. quotations from books, the presentation of data).

- Images, such as graphs, charts and tables, may be used – either within the report or as appendices – to present information as clearly as possible.

- There will often be a balance of evidence, rather than a one-sided presentation, in order to develop the ideas fully and fairly.

- The final paragraph(s) will summarise the main line of reasoning and draw conclusions.

Thus the purpose of a report is to present information that is relevant and accurate, in a clearly structured, fair and balanced way.

THE STRUCTURE OF WRITING

Paragraphing

Paragraphing is a way of helping the reader to follow what is written. It breaks up the text into more readable sections, and shows how the subject develops from one idea to another. Paragraphs normally contain several sentences but, where the sense demands it, a paragraph may be only one or two sentences long. *I will now change paragraph in order to move on to a new aspect of paragraphing.*

When planning to write, it is sometimes useful to think in terms of paragraphs – giving each main point its own paragraph.

Paragraphs may be separated either by indenting the first line by 1–2 cm, like this one, or by double line spacing between paragraphs, like most of the paragraphs in this book. Unless there is a 'house style', choose whichever you prefer, but be consistent; don't change style within the same document (unless you do it deliberately for effect).

Page layout

Page layout can be very important in helping readers to follow your ideas. It is particularly important when you wish to be very clear or persuasive. Think about:

> The length of paragraphs – do you let them wander on for too long?

> Indentation – can you enhance clarity by indenting, as I am doing now with these points?

> Do you need to leave more white space on the page so as not to overwhelm the reader with writing?

Do you need to leave more white space on the page so as not to overwhelm the reader with writing?

Highlighting

There are a number of ways to highlight and draw attention to key points. **One is to use bold, as here.** Examples of other devices include:

• using asterisks or bullet points

– using dashes

underlining

USING CAPITAL LETTERS

enclosing words in a box

The use of word processors has greatly increased the ease of highlighting parts of documents. However, use these devices with discretion – it is possible to overdo them and make the document more difficult to follow.

S T Y L E

Style in what you wear is about expressing your personality with flair. In writing too it is possible to express yourself with more or less style through your choice of words and how you structure what you write. Of course, as with clothes, style is a matter of taste and opinion, but it is important, especially at level 3 and above, to think about the style in which you write.

For instance, which of the following sentences do **you** prefer?

For me work was a new environment, being in school all those years.

or

After being in school all those years, going to work put me in a new environment.

In my opinion, the style of the second version is better. I think it is clearer.

Here is another example:

As I lay at my ease, I looked out over the far Southern sea sinking to sleep in the dusk.

Do you think this is stylish?

Personally, I think there are too many sibilants (the repeated 's' sounds) and I find the idea of the 'sea sinking' unhelpful. I think of sinking in the sea, rather than the sea sinking. However, the very next sentence is better:

The glistening and sparkling of the water passed away – the sea became a great bale of grey-blue silk, soft, smooth, dreamy, like the garment of a sorceress queen.

(Gordon, 1912)

I like the style of this, although I think the sentence could have ended after 'dreamy' – I don't think the last phrase adds to the effectiveness of the sentence. What do you think?

There are no definite 'rules' governing style, but you should consider the impact of your style on the reader. Ask a friend to read your work. Does it have the impact you would like? Is the style appropriate for the audience? For example, the style of a letter applying for a job may be quite different from that of a report for your colleagues of what was decided at a meeting.

Imaginative uses of language

Words – like clothes– can become overused and lose their freshness. Consider words like 'good' and 'nice'. When someone says, 'We had a nice holiday', what are they actually conveying? That the beach was clean and the sea warm? The food was varied and well prepared? They met a lot of friendly people? 'Nice' conveys none of this – it is vague and lacks impact.

 STOP AND THINK
Are there words or expressions that you overuse?

Language may be used in imaginative ways to express information more clearly and forcefully. You may compare one thing with another – 'He's as noisy as a cricket'; 'She is as lithe as a cat'. These are similes. You may use words in ways that are not literally true – 'She is a treasure trove of bright ideas'; 'They left us high and dry'. These are metaphors. Sometimes, like the last example, a metaphor can lose its freshness and power to impress; it becomes clichéd through overuse and loses touch with its literal meaning – in this case the image of a boat stranded by the outgoing tide.

We all use metaphorical language every day. Fiction writers are often particularly skilful at using language in imaginative and fresh ways. Here is an example from Shakespeare's *Hamlet*. Ophelia believes that Hamlet has gone mad. She says, 'Now see that noble and most sovereign reason, like sweet bells jangled, out of tune and harsh.' (Act III, scene i, line 165).

This is an example of an extended metaphor. Here is another example, intended to express information forcefully and memorably:

> Earth is 4,600 million years old. Imagine it as a woman of 46 years. We know nothing about the first 7 years of her life. At 42 she began to flower. Dinosaurs appeared when she was 45. Eight months ago mammals appeared. In the middle of last week apes evolved into humanoid creatures. People like us have been around for 4 hours. In the last hour we have developed agriculture. The Industrial Revolution happened one minute ago.
>
> In the last 60 seconds we have caused the extinction of thousands of species by polluting and destroying rivers, sea, forest and the air.
>
> Will the Earth live to be 47?
>
> We are destroying her; only we can save the Earth.

THE IMPORTANCE OF DRAFTING

A very skilled writer may sometimes finish complex documents in one attempt. However, most people, most of the time, especially if they wish to express complex ideas or opinions with clarity, have to re-draft at least once. Re-drafting is not a sign of weakness as a writer. It shows that thought and practice are needed for most writing beyond the routine.

If you use a word processor it is comparatively easy to

A very skilled writer may sometimes finish complex documents in one attempt.

re-draft, although many people prefer to use pencil and paper for drafting, and only type their final version. Do whatever you prefer – it is the power of your mind in re-drafting that matters, not the power of your processor.

! **STOP AND THINK**
How often do you re-draft your work?

THE MECHANICS OF THE ENGLISH LANGUAGE

Who's afraid of grammar?

Grammar is a word that terrifies some people. It refers to the 'rules' or conventions that govern how words are put together to make sense. Many of these conventions are known intuitively by people

brought up to speak a language. English speakers simply know that 'The cat sat on the mat' is a grammatically correct sentence, whereas 'Sat the mat the cat on' does not make sense because it is ungrammatical. Each word is correct, but the word order is wrong.

So, grammar is nothing to be afraid of. It simply brings out, in the form of more explicit 'rules' or conventions, what most people know already. You may ask yourself then, why bother with 'rules' if most people already know them?

Sometimes, because people ignore the 'rules', they do not make themselves clear. Pointing this out can help avoid similar problems in future. For example, the sentence 'The student stroked a cat <u>in a blue shirt</u>' breaks the 'rule' of grammar that words that belong together should be placed together. The sentence should be written: 'The student <u>in a blue shirt</u> stroked the cat.' This is a light-hearted example (and jokes often depend on bending the normal rules of language). Bear in mind, however, that lawyers make a living out of sentences that are ambiguous and open to interpretation.

A word of warning

The structures of all languages are very complex and change over time. The word 'rules' is in inverted commas to show that the rules are not inflexible, absolute rules but conventions or guides to what should happen most of the time. This is why in Performance Criteria 3 for ELEMENT 2: PRODUCE WRITTEN MATERIAL, you are required to use grammar that follows *standard conventions*, not rules.

Different dialects of any language, including English, have different grammatical conventions. For instance:

'I ain't never seen him.'

'I done it.'

'Stupid you ain't.'

are all grammatical in *non-standard* English. In *standard* English, for the core skill of Communication (i.e. the English that is most closely associated with education, the professions and formal documents) the sentences would be written:

'I have never seen him.'

'I did it.'

'You are not stupid.'

When speaking it is often acceptable (or even expected) that we will use non-standard forms of grammar, whereas when writing for professional purposes it is usually expected that we will use standard English grammar. However, even the grammar conventions of standard English change with time. For example, the word 'data' is plural, and therefore should take a plural verb (e.g. 'The data are clear'). But in fact it is now acceptable to break the 'rule' and to write, 'The data is clear'.

Language is always changing

Language is ever-changing because human beings are ever-changing. Dynamic societies, such as those of the English-speaking world today, give rise to many new words and language conventions.

To illustrate the way that words change, consider that the word 'glamour' has its origins in the word 'grammar'. 'Grammar' originally referred to writing and the letters of the alphabet. The word gradually developed to refer to learning itself (from which derived 'grammar school'). From 'grammar', meaning learning, developed 'grammar', meaning occult learning or magic. Eventually this changed slightly to 'glamour', which in turn began a process of development as a word in its own right. Today the meaning of 'glamour' as magic has been forgotten but you can still sense this older meaning if you think of glamour as 'bewitching beauty'.

Word classes

Words may be classified, according to their use in sentences, into:

Nouns: car, job, justice, France

Pronouns: it, he, who

Adjectives: large, interesting, green

Verbs: run, speak, think

Adverbs: slowly, positively, happily

Prepositions: over, under, on

Conjunctions: and, but, because

Interjections: damn, blimey

It is important to remember that you speak and write using these parts of speech all the time. It may help you to be able to identify and name these elements

It may help you to be able to identify and name these elements of sentences, but this is not essential for their effective use.

of sentences, but this is not essential for their effective use.

Sentence structure

A sentence is a group of words that makes sense without the need to add further words. For instance, 'The sat on the mat' is not a sentence, 'The cat sat on the mat' is.

Keep control of the length of sentences. Don't let them ramble on so that the meaning gets lost. Get a friend to check your work for clarity. Most of all, *make sure that your sentences make sense.*

Sentences come in many sizes and shapes, but they all share the same basic characteristics, because of their function. Most sentences contain three elements : subject, verb and object e.g.:

   I (subject) like (verb) it (object)

Sentences do not always have an object – The child laughs. Time flies. – are sentences.

Sometimes, part of a sentence is 'understood'. Thus 'Like it!' can be a sentence because the subject 'I' is *understood.* Similarly, if you look again at the second paragraph of this section, one sentence reads: 'Keep control of the length of sentences.' 'Keep control' is the verb; 'of the length of sentences' is the object. The subject is 'You', but this is *understood.* However, if I had written 'You of the length of sentences', it

would not be a sentence, because it doesn't make sense without the missing element – the verb. Most sentences are built around verbs, and it is this element that is sometimes missed by people who have difficulty with writing.

It is not always easy to recognise the elements of a sentence, but you can tell when an essential element is missing because the words do not make sense together. However, you do not have to unpick sentences to see how they are made up, any more than you need to take a car apart in order to be able to drive it. And unpicking sentences can be tricky. For example, sometimes the subject may be mysterious. In 'It is raining in Glasgow', what is 'It'? Similarly, an object can be mysterious, as in '(You) Watch it!' Again, what is 'it'? None the less, you can see that these are sentences because all three elements – subject, verb and object are there. Even the single word 'Enough!' can be a sentence if it is clear from what has been written before what the object is. If , for instance, the subject is 'I', in its full form, the sentence would read 'I have had enough of (whatever it is)'. Similarly, 'No' can be a sentence.

Word order

The order of words in a sentence can affect the meaning. 'The student stroked the cat in a blue shirt' has already been given as an example. Another is, 'The car needs servicing badly', when what was meant was 'The car badly needs servicing'. In everyday speech these ambiguities in meaning often do not matter, because it is quite clear what is actually meant. However, in writing, especially for an unknown audience, it is important to get the word order right, so that there is no room for doubt about the meaning.

Verbs

Verbs are the words around which most sentences are structured. Verbs have been called 'doing words', because most of them are about doing something (e.g. run, write, smile, think). However, some verbs are not about doing, but about a state of affairs (e.g. 'it is easy'; 'I have had enough'; 'I am here'). The important thing to remember is that nearly all sentences should have at least one verb.

Verbs change according to who or what their subject is. Take the verb 'like'. Depending on who is doing

the liking, it is written (the technical term is 'conjugated') like this:

I like

You like ·

S/he likes

We like

You (plural) like

They like

Most verbs in the present tense add an 's' in the third person singular (i.e. when the verb refers to she or he or it). Other examples are: I smile – she smiles; you talk – he talks; we grow – it grows.

By listening to people using language, children absorb the structures used. In most cases this leads to them using sentence structures that are grammatically correct, because most people, most of the time use these structures without the need for conscious thought. However, if a person absorbs speech habits that are not grammatically correct in standard English then these may easily become a fixed habit. In some non-standard uses of English people may say, 'She smile', rather than 'She smiles', or 'He talk', rather than 'He talks'. While in everyday speech this may be perfectly acceptable (or even expected), in writing, especially for professional purposes, it is necessary to use standard English grammar.

Verbs also change with *tense*, depending on, for example, whether they refer to present, past or future events. Thus:

I like (present); I liked (past); I will like (future)

In the past and future tenses the form of the verb does *not* change with person:

I liked   I will like

He liked   She will like

Active and passive sentences

'Nurses look after patients' is an active sentence; whereas 'Patients are looked after by nurses' is a passive sentence. If you wish your writing to sound direct and forceful it is preferable to use active sentences – they tend to be shorter and clearer. Passive sentences are sometimes preferred in formal documents because they sound weightier. Here are

some other examples of the difference between active and passive sentence constructions:

The trainee designed the logo. (active)

The logo was designed by the trainee. (passive)

The wheel was turned by the engineer. (passive)

The engineer turned the wheel. (active)

Switching tense

Sometimes writers change tense without meaning to, and switch from past to future or present in ways they do not intend and that confuse the reader:

I looked (*past*) in the window. I open (*present*) the door. I saw (*past*) a man I recognised (*past*).

Here the reader is being given an account of an event in the past and the use of the present tense ('I open') is confusing.

If the writer deliberately decides to use the present tense to describe an event in the past, in order to make it more immediate, it can be very effective:

I look in the window. I open the door. I see a man I recognise.

Here *every* verb is in the present tense. The important thing is to be in control of your writing, and not to switch tenses in ways that may blur your intended meaning.

Agreement

A common mistake is to break the agreement rule (i.e. that the verb should 'agree' with the subject) and to say, for instance, 'We <u>was</u> disappointed with the result', or 'We <u>was</u> happy'. This may sound perfectly acceptable when speaking informally. However, when speaking in an interview, or when writing, it is more appropriate to stick to the rule that noun and verb agree – 'We <u>were</u> disappointed with the result'; 'We <u>were</u> happy'.

There are some words (e.g. 'family', 'class') that can be regarded as either plural or singular. Thus it is correct to write either: 'My family is coming', or 'My family are coming'; 'The class is going', or 'The class are going'.

Split infinitives

The infinitive of a verb is its basic form – 'to win', 'to go', 'to climb'. Putting words between 'to' and the

verb can sometimes sound awkward: 'It is wise to in advance do some preparation' sounds clumsy compared to 'It is wise to do some preparation in advance'; whereas 'To boldly go where no one has gone before' may be a perfectly acceptable split infinitive. This is a matter of opinion and personal preference about which you should be aware.

Of or have?

The verb 'have', in for example, 'I should have known better' is sometimes pronounced 'of'. This has led to some writers writing 'of' instead of 'have', even though there is no verb 'to of'. It is grammatically correct to use 'have'.

Nouns and pronouns

A noun is a word that names (e.g. refers to a thing or abstract idea, person, or place). Examples of nouns are:

> names of objects, big or small (car, book, mouse, sky)
>
> words that refer to ideas (justice, mercy, freedom)
>
> names of people and places (London, Joanne, Paris, Matthew)
>
> words that refer to knowledge (philosophy, plumbing, communication)

Nouns are often preceded by an article ('a' or 'the'), although some abstract nouns (e.g. 'justice') may stand alone.

Most sentences have nouns in them, or the nouns are understood, as in 'Stop it!' where the noun (e.g. 'John, stop it!') is clear from the context.

It can be repetitious to use nouns all the time, so we often substitute pronouns for them. An example is, 'When Mr Davis came into the room he was warmly welcomed', which sounds less clumsy than 'When Mr Davis came into the room Mr Davis was warmly welcomed'. Examples of pronouns are: 'he', 'she', 'it', 'they', 'their'. When using pronouns, you must make sure that it is clear to which nouns they refer. Read over your work, or get a friend to check it, to ensure that you have achieved clarity.

These, those and them

'These' and 'those' are examples of demonstrative pronouns, used to point out something. If what is pointed out is near, 'these' is used (e.g. 'These apples are juicy'). If what is pointed out is farther off, 'those' is used (e.g. 'Those hills in the distance').

Avoid using the personal pronoun 'them' when 'these' or 'those' should be used. Sentences such as 'Them apples are juicy'; 'Them hills in the distance' are ungrammatical in standard English.

I or me?

Should you write:

> 'Mia and **I** went to the pictures', or 'Mia and **me** went to the pictures'?
>
> 'Joanne looked at Mia and **I**', or 'Joanne looked at Mia and **me**'?

The 'rule' is that if the pronoun ('I' or 'me') is the subject of a sentence, 'I' should be used; if it is the object of the sentence, 'me' should be used. In the first example 'Mia and I' is the subject and so 'I' is correct. Another way of thinking about it is that, without Mia, the sentence would be 'I went to the pictures'. This sounds right. Adding Mia does not change anything.

 STOP AND THINK!
Which of the sentences in the second example is correct? Take out the words 'Mia and'. Which of the remaining sentences sounds correct? 'Joanne looked at I' or 'Joanne looked at me'?

The correct sentence is 'Joanne looked at Mia and me', because 'Mia and me' is the object of the sentence, therefore, 'me', rather than 'I', is correct.

Adjectives and adverbs

You can add adjectives and adverbs to sentences to tell the reader more about the subject, the object or the verb. The sentence:

> The man (subject) likes (verb) ice-cream (object)

can be extended by, for example, adding:

> an adjective to the subject: The *smart* man
>
> an adverb to the verb: *really* likes
>
> an adjective to the object: *vanilla* ice-cream

creating the sentence:

> The smart man really likes vanilla ice-cream.

Comparative adjectives

'More simple' or 'simpler'? Sometimes people find it difficult to decide which is preferable. What do you think?

Very often it sounds more harmonious to use the shorter construction. 'The text was simpler than she expected' sounds better than 'The text was more simple than she expected'. So you have:

simple	simpler	simplest
cool	cooler	coolest

However, some comparisons need to use the word 'more' (e.g. 'She is more beautiful than her sister', rather than 'She is beautifuler than her sister') so you have:

beautiful	more beautiful	most beautiful
satisfied	more satisfied	most satisfied

Positions of prepositions

The last sentence in the paragraph on split infinitives could have been written, 'This is a matter of opinion and personal preference that you should be aware of.' But there has long been a 'rule' in English that a sentence should not end with a preposition (words such as: on, by, for, through, with, of).

Once again this is a matter of opinion and personal preference. Winston Churchill, British Prime Minister during the Second World War, made fun of the 'rule' by showing how convoluted a sentence can become if you try to apply it. Instead of writing the direct and harmonious sentence, 'This is something I will not put up with', he wrote, 'This is something up with which I will not put.'

Who or whom?

In very formal English usage, 'whom' rather than 'who' is used after a preposition, or when it forms the object rather than the subject of a sentence. So, for example, 'Our leader, in whom we believe' (after preposition); 'He is the man who did it' ('He' is the subject of the sentence) but 'He is the man whom I met yesterday' ('I' is the subject and 'He' is the object of the sentence).

However, this 'rule' is disappearing from everyday use and, if applied, can sometimes sound clumsy or even faintly ridiculous. Most people would now say,

'He is the man who I met yesterday'. People would also probably break two 'rules' (who/whom *and* preposition) and say, 'Our leader, who we believe in'.

That, who, which and what

Relative pronouns, such as 'that', 'who', and 'which', are used to begin relative clauses (a clause is a group of words in a sentence with their own subject and verb).

There are two kinds of relative clauses.

Some clauses explain something in the main part of the sentence, without which the sentence would not make complete sense. These begin with 'that', e.g:

This is the song *that* John Lennon wrote.

She is the best singer *that* I have ever heard.

Sometimes, as in these examples, it is possible to drop the word 'that' without altering the meaning.

The second kind of relative clause gives additional information in a sentence that already makes sense. These begin with 'who' ('whom') or 'which', e.g.:

Julie Tullis, *who* climbed K2, was a brave woman.

Here, the main sentence 'Julie Tullis was a brave woman' could make sense on its own, 'who climbed K2' gives additional information. Here is another example:

I gave him £10, *which* was all I could afford.

Notice that 'that' may refer to people or things (song or singer), whereas 'who' usually refers to people (Julie Tullis) and 'which usually refers to things (£10).

The relative pronoun 'what' is sometimes used in non-standard English instead of 'who' (e.g. 'It's the rich what gets the fun; it's the poor what gets the blame'; 'He's the bloke what done it'). However, in standard English the pronoun 'who' should be used.

Less or fewer?

There is often confusion about whether you should write 'less' or 'fewer' in a sentence such as, 'There are less/fewer cars on the road'. The convention is that if a number of objects is being referred to, rather than an amount, use 'fewer'. So it should be 'There are fewer cars on the road'.

However, you would say, 'He takes less milk on cornflakes', not 'He takes fewer milk on cornflakes', because you have an amount of milk, rather than individual bits of milk.

Research has shown that the use of the word 'man' implies that women are excluded.

Gender

Referring to both men and women when writing the sentence 'Each person should remain seated at. . . desk', should you write 'his', 'her', 'his/her', or 'their' desk? When 'his' is used, it is claimed that women are somehow included, in the same way as they are assumed to be included in the word 'man' when it is used to refer to human beings in general. But research has shown that this is not the case and that it implies that women are excluded; people tend to think only of *men* when 'man' is used (e.g. 'the man in the street', 'man-made'). Repeated use of 'his/her' is clumsy, so it is acceptable to write 'their desk', even though 'their', being plural, would normally take a plural noun, 'desks'.

DOUBLE NEGATIVES

In some non-standard English dialects it is acceptable to say sentences such as:

I didn't say nothing.

which contain two negatives that, in a sense, cancel one another out. Literally, this sentence means 'I said something'. In fact the context, or occasion when it is used, and the tone of voice can make plain what is meant. However, when writing for professional purposes this would be seen as ungrammatical. In standard English it should read: 'I said nothing', or 'I didn't say anything'.

PUNCTUATION

Punctuation has two main purposes:

to enable written language to be read in a way that increases the reader's understanding;

to give an indication of the sounds of speech.

The meaning of spoken words is made clear in a number of ways (e.g. loudness, pitch, speed, etc.). Think what different meanings the simple words, 'Open the door' can convey depending on how they are spoken (e.g. they could imply 'I have a present for you'; 'I'm fed up standing here'; 'This is the Police'). In writing it is necessary to punctuate in order to convey some of these possible meanings (e.g. 'Open the door?', or 'Open the door!')

Capital letters

Capitals may be used to emphasise text. It is a matter of personal choice whether you choose to emphasise writing in this way. For example, because PUNCTUATION is a new and important section of this guide, it has been emphasised by the use of capital letters.

Capital letters are also used in the following ways:

- First letter of a sentence

- The personal pronoun, 'I'

- Beginning of direct speech – she said, 'Hello.'

- First letter of a proper noun, such as:

  days of the week – Sunday, Monday
  months of the year – December, January
  people's names – Mia, Hannah, Matthew
  place names – Oxford, New York
  titles of books, films, etc. – *Jaws*, *Red Dwarf*

- Titles of people or organisations – the Prime Minister, the Queen, the National Society for the Prevention of Cruelty to Children (NSPCC)

- People's initials – J.R.R. Tolkien

- Abbreviations – NSPCC, NCVQ, BBC, AA

Full stops

Full stops mark the end of sentences, unless another mark (! ?) is used instead. Without the use of full stops it might be difficult to follow the meaning of what is written, e.g

> Jesse Boot sold medicines cheaply in 1892 he began to make drugs by 1900 he had 126 shops

STOP AND THINK
Where could you put a full stop to clarify the meaning?

Answer: **Jesse Boot sold medicines cheaply. In 1892 he began to make drugs. By 1900 he had 126 shops.**

The comma

Commas help to make sentences easier to read and clearer, by separating them into parts (clauses, phrases, lists). Consider the sentence:

> Peter a psychiatrist believes that handled well organised activities can help a child.

The meaning of this sentence can be clarified by adding commas.

STOP AND THINK
Where would you add commas?

The basic sentence is, 'Peter believes that organised activities can help a child.' The other parts of the sentence are additions that provide further information. They can be marked off from the basic part by commas, 'Peter, a psychiatrist, believes that, handled well, organised activities can help a child.'

In this way the sentence becomes easier to read and to understand.

Semi-colons and colons

A full stop brings a sentence to a halt; a comma produces a pause; a semi-colon can be thought of as half way between, producing a longer pause than a comma. It is used, like the comma, to help the reader understand the structure of the sentence. Consider this lengthy sentence:

> Matthew described what he carried in his pocket: 'A whistle, in case I meet a wolf; a clip, in case I meet a crocodile; and a small, plastic zebra, in case I wish to cross a road.'

Here you can see how the use of commas and semi-colons helps to break up the sentence and emphasise its meaning. In the sentence a colon is used to introduce Matthew's list. It is also used at the end of the sentence before to introduce the example.

Here is another example of the use of colons to introduce a list, and semi-colons to separate the different parts:

> 'Even fairy-stories as a whole have three faces: the Mystical towards the Supernatural; the Magical towards Nature; and the Mirror of scorn and pity towards Man.'
>
> (Tolkien, 1975)

Hyphens

A hyphen is a sign (-) used to join the parts of a compound word (e.g. 'forget-me-not'). Some words (e.g. 'headmaster') have become one word after a period of being hyphenated (head-master).

Hyphens should be distinguished from dashes – which are longer and may be used instead of commas (as here) or brackets.

Brackets

Brackets are signs – ( ) { } [ ] – used in pairs to mark off examples (or other additional material) from the main part of a sentence.

Material within brackets should be punctuated normally. The next section, on *Inverted commas* has a number of examples of the use of brackets.

Inverted commas

In the examples above, inverted commas have been used to show that the words were spoken or written by someone other than the writer of this book. In the first example Matthew spoke the words about what was in his pocket; in the second example the words were written by J.R.R. Tolkien in a book called *Tree and Leaf.*

All the actual words spoken or written should be inside the inverted commas, but if these words are interrupted by, for example, *he said,* these words are not direct speech (i.e. they are not what someone actually said, but are an explanation or commentary about who said the words). For example:

> The doctor looked concerned (commentary), 'Please take three of these tablets,' (direct speech) he said (commentary), 'and drink plenty of water.' (direct speech)

Notice that each sentence of direct speech begins as all sentences should, with a capital letter, and the punctuation of the direct speech is inside the inverted commas. In other words, punctuate what is said in the normal way. If you interrupt what is actually said by words such as *he said; she asked*, then these words should be suitably punctuated, for example:

> 'What are these tablets called?', she asked,
> 'They're big enough to be Flying Saucers.'

The best place to see the use of inverted commas for direct speech is in novels, although a few novelists dispense with inverted commas altogether, preferring to show speech by other means. Here is an example from James Joyce's *Portrait of the Artist*:

> The fellows talked together in little groups.
>
> One fellow said:
>
> – They were caught near the Hill of Lyons.
> (Joyce, 1916)

Here, Joyce has introduced the direct speech by a colon followed, on the next line, by a dash. However, it is still clear what is commentary and what is actual direct speech.

Another point to note about writing direct speech is that the convention is to start a new paragraph each time the speaker changes.

Reported speech

Sometimes it is preferable to report what has been spoken, rather than to write it out word for word in direct speech.

 STOP AND THINK
Look at the example of the doctor and patient above. If you get rid of the inverted commas and report what has been said, what would you write or say?

Here is a possible report of what was spoken:

> The doctor looked concerned. He asked the patient to take three tablets and to drink lots of water. She looked in alarm at the large, round tablets and asked if they were called Flying Saucers.

If you take the minutes of meetings it can be very tedious to write down people's actual words. It is usually advisable to report what they have said, summarising only important statements and decisions.

? Question marks?

When speaking, it is usually plain that a question is being asked because the pitch of speech changes. Even a single word like 'Hello' can be an exclamation, a question or a grumble, depending on how it is said.

When writing, it is necessary to give the reader extra clues about what the spoken words actually mean. The reader can tell if, 'The tablets will do her good' is a question or a statement by whether or not it is followed by a question mark.

! Exclamation marks!

The last example could also be written, 'The tablets will do her good!' This has the effect of conveying in writing what would be shown in actual speech by, for example, loudness of voice, rising pitch of voice, and facial expression. It gives the reader a clue to the actual impact and meaning of the words. However, take care not to over-use exclamation marks – if used too much they can give an impression of hysteria.

Apostrophe

One of the most tricky punctuation marks for people to use is the apostrophe. It is used in two ways:

* to show that letters or numbers have been omitted (e.g. it's = it is; can't = can not; don't = do not)

* to show possession (e.g. Mia's jumper; Frank's piano)

However, some words can cause confusion. In 'Its safe to open its cage', which 'its' takes an apostrophe?

The answer is the first, because it is short for 'It is', whereas the second is a word like 'hers', 'ours', 'yours', 'theirs', 'whose', all of which show possession, without need for apostrophes. So if you can substitute 'it is' for 'its', you need to use an apostrophe.

'Susan's gone', and 'Susan's boyfriend' are examples of the use of apostrophe to show omission (Susan has gone) and possession (the boyfriend of Susan).

You can also use an apostrophe if you want to leave some numbers out of a year (e.g. '68 for 1968), but it must be clear what century you are writing about.

The possessive apostrophe and words ending in 's'

Singular nouns add an 's' after the apostrophe – 'Brad's pen'; 'the lion's cage'. This is still true for singular nouns that already end in 's' – the walrus's whiskers. Plural nouns that end in 's' (as most plural nouns do) take the apostrophe alone and do not add a second 's' – 'the Liberals' policies'; 'the lions' cages'. Plural nouns that do not end in 's' follow the normal rule – 'children's shoes'; 'women's issues'. In *every* case, the apostrophe is immediately after what or who is the possessor.

Abbreviations

Abbreviations usually have a full stop after them to show that they have been cut short, for example:

approx. etc. Insp.

However, some abbreviations do not need full stops:

- Contractions (where the middle of the word is omitted and the last letter is retained, such as: Mr, Mrs, Ms, Rd, St, Ave, Dr)

- Capital letters (MP, AA, NCVQ, BBC, UN, EU)

- Acronyms (pronounceable abbreviations, such as NATO, GATT)

- Measurements and quantities (mm, g, p [= pence])

The 'rules' of abbreviation, and punctuation in general, are becoming more relaxed.

SPELLING

Many people worry about the standard of their spelling. Most people make errors from time to time.

United Kingdom Acronym Society, may I help you?

Darwin, for example, in the log of his journey on the *Beagle* spelt 'yacht' as 'yatch', and 'broad' as 'broard'. Spelling English is more difficult than, for example, spelling Spanish. This is because there is not a regular correspondence between the way words sound when spoken, and the way they look on the page when written. 'To', 'two' and 'too' all sound alike; 'plough' and 'rough' have the same ending but are pronounced differently.

Learning to spell correctly is a matter of practice. The more you read and write, the more proficient you will become. However, there are some 'rules' that you can learn to help you, and it is possible, and a good idea, to memorise or keep a note of words that you misspell frequently.

Make use of a good-quality dictionary. This will give you information about the pronunciation of words and which part of speech a word forms (e.g. verb, noun, etc.) as well as the correct spelling. It is usual to look up the 'head word' (or 'root'). For example, if you are uncertain about how to spell 'beginning', then look up 'begin' and you will find words built on this root, including 'beginning'.

Word-processing programs also have spell checks that you can use to improve your work. However, these are no substitute for being able to spell correctly.

A list of words that are frequently misspelled

! STOP AND THINK
Here are some words that may cause difficulty. Ask someone to test you on them. Highlight those you cannot spell correctly and try to learn them. Keep a list of other words that you find difficult to spell.

accelerate	counsellor	professional
accessible	(adviser)	psychological
accommodate	credible	questionnaire
adviser *but*	disappear	queue
advisory	embarrass	representative
aesthetic	exaggerate	responsible
barbecue	familiar	success
beggar	fulfil	sufficient
beginning	gauge	transmit
benefited	literature	vinegar
camera	maintenance	visible
commit	moustache	
committee	necessary	
councillor	occasion	
(member of a	parallel	
council)	possess	

and to think they call US eccentric!!

RULES OF ENGLISH SPELLING

'Rules' of spelling

There are some 'rules' you can try to follow in order to improve your spelling. However, there is no substitute for practising – reading and writing.

Forming plurals

The rule is add 's'. However, there are a number of exceptions:

> words ending in 's', 'x', 'z', 'ch', 'sh' take 'es' – pass/passes; push/pushes

> words ending in 'o' take 'es' – potato/potatoes

> words ending in 'y' become 'ies' – lady/ladies

> words ending in 'f', or 'fe' replace 'f' with 'v' and add 's' – knife/knives (there are some exceptions to this – roof/roofs; belief/beliefs; dwarf/dwarfs)

Some words still use their Latin or Greek endings in the plural:

> words ending in 'is' become 'es' – thesis/theses; crisis/crises; axis/axes

> words ending in 'a' become 'ae' – formula/formulae; penumbra/penumbrae (however, it is becoming more usual to use 'formulas' and 'penumbras').

Of course, some English words are eccentric and follow no rule (e.g. child/children; mouse/mice). This is why it is necessary to become used to writing words – learning rules may not always be of help.

Other 'rules'

The most well known rule of English spelling is that you put 'i' before 'e' except after 'c' (e.g. 'chief', 'friend'). However, there are a number of exceptions (e.g. 'weird', 'seize', 'weir').

Sometimes, 'ce' and 'se' endings are confused (e.g. advice/advise). The rule is that most 'ce' endings are of nouns – 'the advice'; 'se' endings are of verbs – 'to advise'. Similarly, 'the practice/to practise'; 'the licence/to license'.

Often, people get confused with some verb endings – is it 'compelled' or 'compeled'? 'Benefited' or 'benefitted'?

The rule is that if the root word ('compel', 'benefit') has more than one syllable, and the stress is on the last syllable then you double the consonant. So 'compel', because it is a word of more than one syllable, with the stress on the last syllable, doubles the last letter to become 'compelled'. The word 'benefit', on the other hand, has the stress on the first, not the last syllable, so the final letter, 't', is not doubled and the word becomes 'benefited'.

Words that are sometimes confused

Some words cause difficulty because they are similar to other words of different meaning. For example:

> accept/except (I accept the invitation; everyone will go, except Jack)

It is only through using such words a number of times in your writing that you will feel comfortable with them. If you have any difficulty with the words in the list below, write a few sentences in which you try to use them correctly. Get a friend to check over your work. Here are some more examples of sentences that could be written to practise using these words:

> We accept credit cards.

> All the children, except Tom, won a prize.

You can also practise words that are based on 'accept/except':

> The Oscar acceptance speech was witty.

> She took exception to the way he talked to her.

Try these:

affect/effect ('I felt the effect'; 'The new rules will not affect me')

aloud/allowed ('Please read aloud'; 'Smoking is not allowed')

chose/choose ('I chose a red dress' [past tense]; 'I choose you' [present tense])

continual/continuous ('Drip, drip, drip – the leak was continual'; 'There was a continuous flow of water from the broken pipe')

current/currant ('I floated with the current'; 'She ate a currant bun')

dependant/dependent ('My baby is my dependant'; 'Whether we go is dependent on having enough money')

lay/lie ('The dog lay in its basket'; 'Alison said that she would never lie')

Loose/lose ('The tooth was loose'; 'He didn't want to lose it')

new/knew ('The house is new'; 'I knew it all along')

passed/past ('I passed the pub on my way to work'; 'In the past [time] people walked faster'; 'I walked past [position] the pub on my way to work')

practice/practise ('The doctor's practice was busy'; 'Sam practised the piano')

principle/principal ('I object to bullying on principle'; 'the College Principal was a fair woman')

quiet/quite ('The boy was very quiet'; 'He did not know quite what to do')

stationary/stationery ('The train was stationary'; 'I took out some stationery to write a letter')

their/they're/there ('Their coats are hanging up'; 'They're [they are] very heavy'; 'You will find them over there')

to/too ('I am going to Florence'; 'Rebecca is coming too' [i.e. also]; 'He is too eager' [i.e. excessively])

threw/through ('Sam threw the ball for the dog'; 'I can see through you')

were/we're ('We were happy'; 'We're [we are] happy')

who's/whose ('Who's [who is] going to the party?'; 'Whose coat is this?')

your/you're ('Your mother is here'; 'You're [you are] beautiful')

Element 2.3 and 3.3: Use images

Confucius is supposed to have said that 'a picture is worth a thousand words'. Communication is dominated by images – cinema, television, advertising, magazines, and newspapers all make heavy use of images, to the extent that, sometimes, words become secondary or even redundant.

It is often very helpful when writing and speaking to use images to illustrate points that you wish to make. When you do, it is important that the images are in fact relevant to what you say or write, and are not merely padding – PC 1; that they are suited to the audience (e.g. how much will they know about the subject?), the situation (e.g. is it an informal discussion or a formal presentation?) and the purpose of the communication (e.g. to entertain,

persuade, convey ideas accurately?) – PC2; and that they illustrate clearly the points being made (e.g. by being used at an appropriate place in a document or time in a presentation) – PC3.

What sorts of images can I use?

All sorts of images may be used to support writing or speaking. There is no limit to the type of image that may be used, other than that it must satisfy the Performance Criteria for USING IMAGES. Most images are two dimensional (e.g. maps, sketches, pictures) but you may use three-dimensional models (e.g. a scale model of a product or building).

You are expected to be able to select suitable images

(e.g. from material you have read) and to produce your own images, by hand or using a computer, in order to illustrate points that you make in speaking and in writing.

Do you have to be very skilful to use images?

The answer is no. Most people can use images without any problem at all. Schools, colleges and workplaces have all sorts of images readily available: in newspapers, journals, books, and libraries.

If you can't find an appropriate image, it is not difficult to take a photograph; draw a diagram, table or chart; or even to draw a sketch.

 STOP AND THINK
Do you make sufficient use of images to support your speaking and writing? Do you need to experiment with using a wider variety of images?

EXAMPLES OF IMAGES

The names given to particular kinds of image are sometimes interchangeable. Some charts may be called diagrams, some sketches may be called maps, some tables may be called charts. Do not worry about what you call an image, as long as its use helps you to communicate more effectively.

Sketching

Sketching does not require fine artistic skills – even matchstick people can be used to good effect to illustrate or explain a point.

Symbols

A symbol is a mark or conventional sign representing a quality or an idea. We are surrounded by symbols, some of which we scarcely notice as symbols – a lion may represent power and pride; the cross represents Christianity. Symbols can be powerful images. They are often used by advertisers, and in propaganda – think of the registered trademark symbol, the Union Jack, or the Nazi swastika. Here are some examples of symbols:

Do you know what they all mean?

Logos

A logo is an image used as the badge or symbol of an organisation. It should be eye-catching and memorable, because the purpose is to make people more aware of the organisation. Do you recognise these logos?

Panda device © 1986 WWF – World Wide Fund For Nature (formerly World Wildlife Fund)

Diagrams

A diagram is a sketch that shows the main features of a particular object or process. Like many other types of image it is not an accurate portrayal of the object or process, but a simplified image that conveys the main features for the purpose of clear illustration. For example:

3a

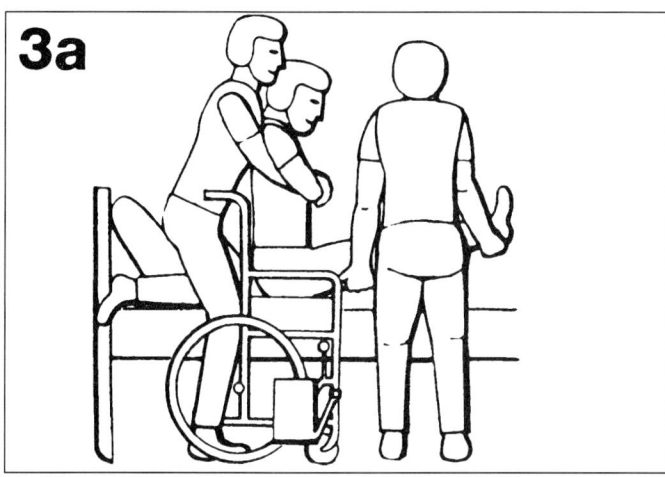

How to lift someone safely

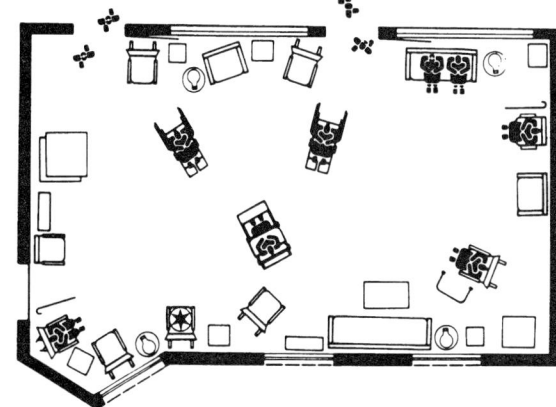

The layout of a building

Charts

There are many types of charts – for example, navigational charts; graphs; sheets of tabulated information. They present information in a 'see-at-a-glance' form.

A temperature chart enables doctors and nurses to see how a patient is progressing over time.

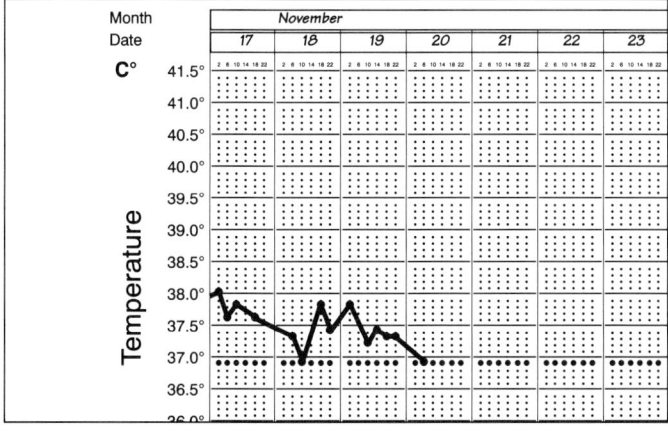

A music chart shows what music is popular at a particular time.

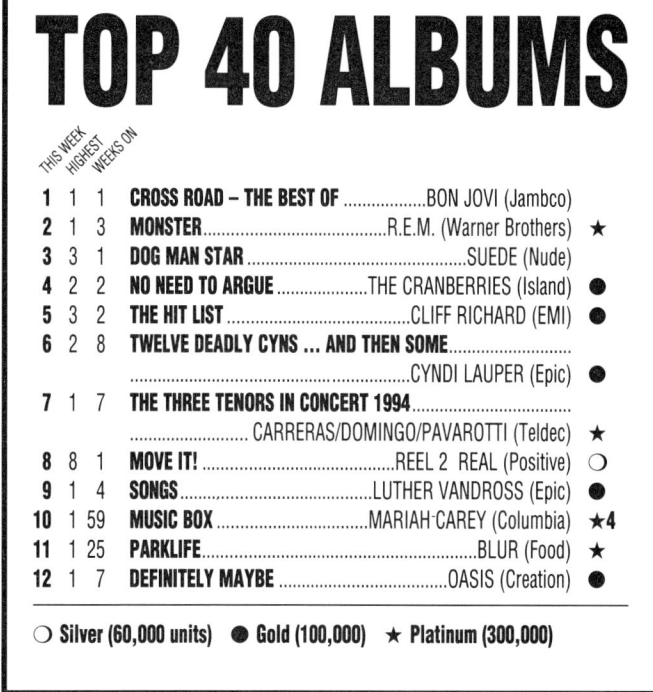

Part of a monthly album chart

A pie chart is useful for showing the different sized divisions (slices) of one complete whole – the pie (e.g. types of hotel in a particular resort). Pie charts can be confusing, however, if there are too many slices.

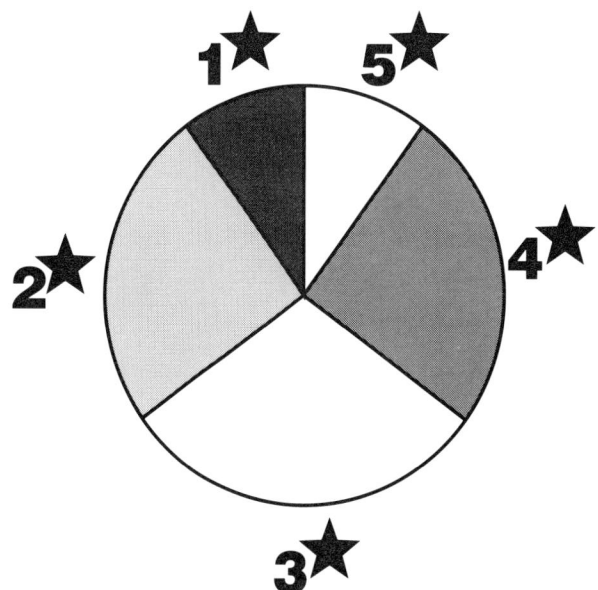

Bar charts (or column charts) tend to be most useful when you want to show selected examples of one factor (e.g. numbers of hotels in selected resorts). They have two axes (one vertical; one horizontal) and you can display as many bars as you wish. Bar charts work best when the differences are not so great as to make the vertical axis very long, or the shorter bars too small to distinguish.

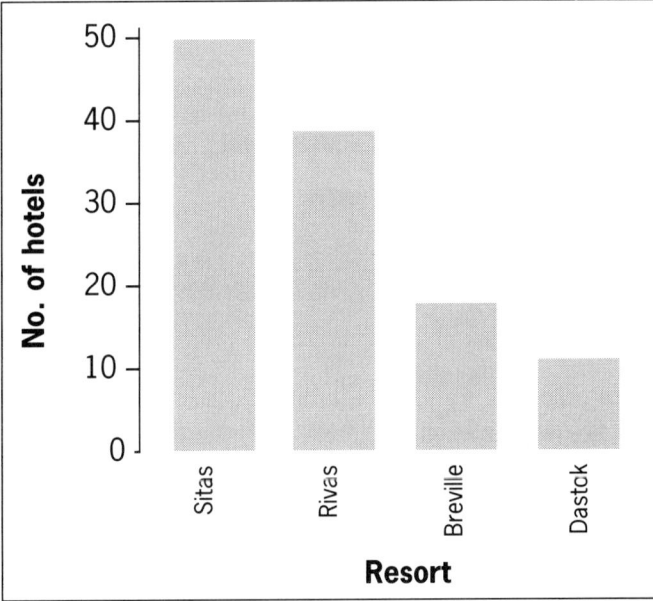

Tables

A table lists facts, numbers, etc., and is usually arranged in columns. The purpose of a table is to provide information to a reader in a form that is easy to read and useful. For example, the Table of Contents of a book enables the reader to go to a particular part without leafing through the entire book.

Here are two examples of tables:

Category	1	2	3	4
Mobility	Fully mobile/ Independent	Uses aids, e.g. zimmer, stick, occ. use of wheelchair	Needs wheelchair. Some use in hands and arms.	Completely immobile. Total care required.
Communication	Is able to see, hear well and speak.	Some difficulty seeing, hearing, speaking, but copes well.	Dysphasic or hard of hearing, or partially sighted.	Aphasic/total deafness, blind. Uses aids – letter/picture cards, speech console

Part of the McLoughlin scale – Mobility and Communication

The table below is a printout from a computer spreadsheet program, which automatically labels rows and columns with numbers and letters, for easy reference to each 'cell'. Spreadsheets are frequently used for business and accounting purposes.

	A	B	C	D	E	F	G
1		Jan	Feb	Mar	Apr	May	Jun
2							
3	Hardware sales	2300	1500	950	1700	2000	2200
4	Software sales	100	70	100	375	500	375
5	**Total sales**	2400	1570	1050	2075	2500	2575
6	Direct costs	800	650	700	700	675	725
7	Indirect costs	20	35	20	40	60	30
8	Overheads	350	70	100	200	100	200
9	**Total costs**	1170	755	820	940	835	955
10	**INCOME**	1230	815	230	1135	1665	1620

Photographs

A photograph is, literally, 'light writing' (photo = light; graph = writing). Photographs enable us to depict people, places and events that would be very time-consuming to portray in words. It is neither difficult nor expensive to produce a few photographs to illustrate what you wish to say or write, especially if you collaborate with others to share the costs.

Slides can be particularly effective to illustrate a presentation.

Video can also be used but it can be difficult and time-consuming to produce even a short video of suitable quality.

Overhead projector transparencies are easy to use so long as you bear in mind that the further people are from the screen, the larger images need to be; and that you should use few words or images because it is tedius to try and read a lot of material from a screen.

Maps

A map is a representation of the whole or some part of the physical world. It simplifies what it represents in order to help the user understand the image. (If the London Underground map showed the correct bends and turns of the tunnels, and the correct scaled distances, it would either be too huge to hold,

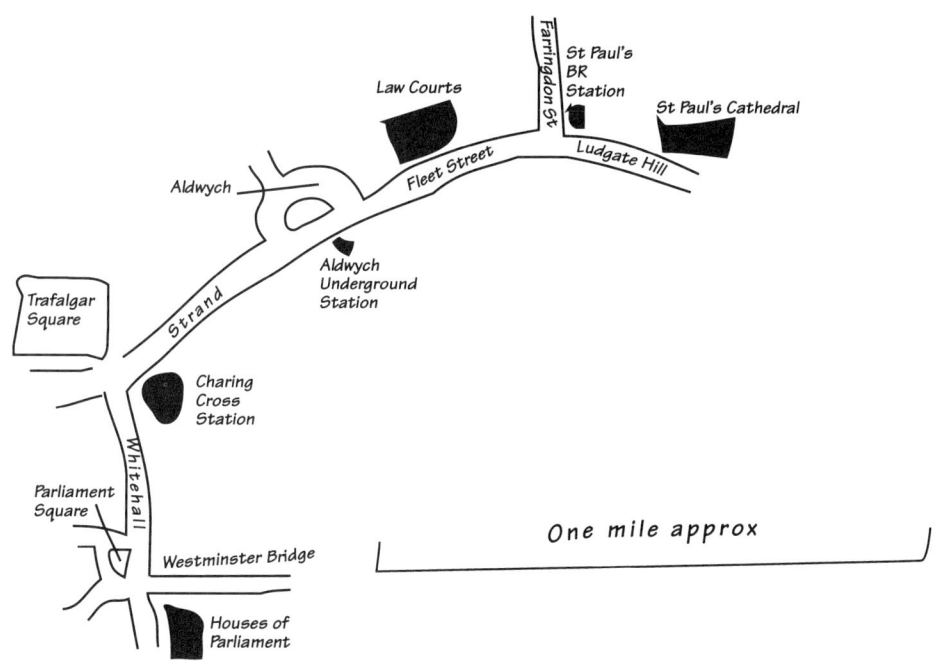

A simple hand-drawn map to show the route between St Paul's and the Houses of Parliament

or so complicated that no one would be able to follow it.)

So, if you are drawing a map, remember to keep it simple. Only put on major landmarks or other means by which users can orientate themselves; give a scale (is it 10 metres or 10 miles?). Remember, it only has to be fit for its purpose – not a work of art, or an accurate depiction of the world!

Element 2.4 and 3.4: Read and respond to written materials

Writing and reading are relatively recent human skills. Human beings have existed for millions of years, but the earliest examples of writing date back only a few thousand years. The need to keep records of business transactions seems to have been the spur to invent writing and its accompanying skill of reading.

The types of reading that are emphasised in Communication are linked to this earliest and continuing need to use language to record information and make it accessible in books, articles, reports, letters, memos and other formats.

Reading is carried out for a purpose, such as to obtain information, feedback, ideas, opinions and instructions. Having read material you then *use* it in some way, which is why the title of the element is *Read and <u>respond</u> to materials*.

Reading, like writing and all other skills, can be improved by practice. If you wish to play the guitar well, or cook to a high standard, you need to practice. Some people become frustrated by their lack of skill at reading and blame this on either themselves ('I'm stupid'), or on the writing ('It's boring'), when the truth is that they don't read often enough to build up a high level of skill. So, if you wish to read better, read often (whatever interests you – books, magazines, newspapers) and, like magic, your reading will improve!

Level

Whether a piece of writing is at LEVEL 2 or LEVEL 3 for the purpose of Communication depends on three factors:

- how complex the subject is – is it routine or non-routine; straightforward or complex?

- how complex the structure of the document is – is it an obvious and familiar structure; or complex and less familiar?

- the kind of help available to understand the document – is it provided for you; or do you have to seek out help yourself?

Thus, a letter or report on a subject that is familiar to you, when help is available from tutors and/or books, will be at LEVEL 2; whereas a book or lengthy report on a complex subject, when you have to seek out clarification on your own initiative, will be at LEVEL 3.

Remember that the level resides in the writing and not in the reader – someone used to reading scientific reports may read them with ease, yet the reports are still at LEVEL 3 or above; another person may find it very difficult to read a simple letter, and the letter will still only be at LEVEL 2.

UNDERSTANDING IMAGES

There is a well-known saying – 'There are lies, damned lies, and statistics'. Care needs to be taken when interpreting images, especially those that present statistics. Imagine a banner headline – CRIME FIGURE SOARS! – accompanied by this graph:

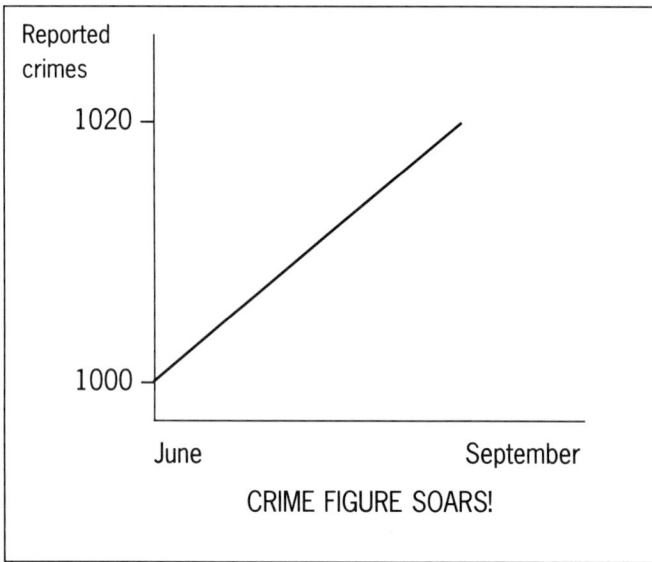

CRIME FIGURE SOARS!

However, if you look at the vertical scale, you will see that there are only 20 more crimes, from 1000, to 1020, which is not as dramatic as the headline suggests. Similarly, if the horizontal time scale were to be extended to show a 12-month, rather than a 3-month period, it would be seen that crime actually fell and has not reached its former level:

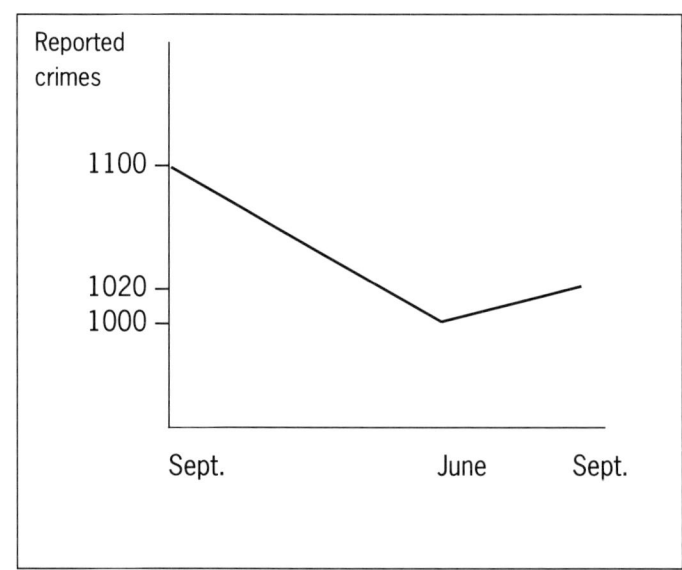

Thus, the choice of vertical and horizontal scales can affect the meaning of a graph very profoundly. When reading this sort of image it is necessary to pay close attention to the value of the scales to avoid being misled.

A general principle for interpreting images is *read the labels*. This applies not only to graphs and charts, but to many other images too. For instance, say you come across the following:

Unless you read the label, or have come across the image before, you may misinterpret it.

The label reads 'Risk of long hair being drawn into air inlet'.

Reading the labelling on diagrams is particularly important for electrical wiring diagrams, when a misreading can lead to death or serious injury.

If you do not understand an image, consult another person.

BEING SELECTIVE ABOUT WHAT YOU READ

There is so much information available today that no one can possibly read more than a tiny fraction of what has been written. You have to be selective – first of all about which books, articles, etc. to read, and secondly, about how carefully you want to read what you select.

If you wish to research a particular topic there may be a range of ways of gathering information (e.g. questioning people or conducting experiments). A very effective way of gathering information is to read what other people have written about the topic. You may know someone who can give you advice about what to read or can lend you material, or you may need to use a library.

STOP AND THINK
Do you use suitable techniques to select relevant information? Do you know how to use a library effectively?

Using a library

Libraries were opened shortly after the invention of writing. The first public library was opened at Athens in 330 BC. Public libraries and college libraries are treasure houses of information and ideas, and it is worth finding out how to use them efficiently. Browsing along the shelves can be an interesting way to spend some time, but if you wish to find information quickly, it is necessary to know how to use the library's classification system.

There are two main classification systems in current use: the Universal Decimal Classification (formerly the Dewey Decimal system), and the Library of Congress Classification. Every library has a catalogue to show readers which books and journals are available. A catalogue may be on cards, microfiche or a database. The most effective way to learn about the system in your library is to use it. Most librarians are happy to explain the system and help people find their way about – just ask.

Here is an example of a library search in a large library using an on-line database:

> **Step 1**: Decide which topic you wish to find out about (the more specific you can be, the more likely it is that you will find what you need).
>
> Let us assume the topic is language.

Step 2: The information on screen reads:

```
On-line catalogue main menu
Please type one of the following letters and
press RETURN
   T   for Title search
   A   for Author and name search
   K   for searching Keywords within titles
   S   for Subject search
   C   for Class number search
```

> You decide to type **K**, to search for the keyword 'language'. When you have typed in the keyword, the program informs you that:

There are 3030 references matching your enquiry

> You could scroll through all 3030 titles, which would take a long time, or, the computer tells you, press **C** to continue the search. When you do this, the program offers you a number of alternatives, including:

1. Continue with another word to NARROW your search

> You type in 'education', because you are interested in language in education. The program informs you that:

There are 941 references matching your enquiry

> You decide to narrow the search even further by using another option:

4. Restrict your search by date of publication

> You type in '1988' – to request titles of books about language in education published in 1988 or after. The program informs you that:

There are 210 references matching your enquiry

> This is still too many, so you narrow the search still further by using option 1 (narrow your search with another word) and typing 'English'. The program informs you that:

There are 19 references matching your enquiry

> You then scroll through the references and request more information about the second book on the list. The program informs you of the title, date of publication, author (in this case the Department for Education), publisher (in this case Her Majesty's Stationery Office), and classification number, in the

Universal Decimal Classification, under which you will find the publication shelved:

English Language and Education, 1991
Great Britain, Department for Education, London, HMSO
372.4/GRE

You may then go to the shelf where the 372 classification books are stored, take down the publication and dip into it to see whether it is worth borrowing.

This process need only take a few minutes once you are used to it. Imagine, instead, having to search a large library for a book on English language and education without the help of a catalogue – it may take you days.

Smaller libraries may not have an on-line catalogue system and you may have to search a card index. Some indexes are arranged alphabetically by author; others by subject; others by class number. Once again, the best way to familiarise yourself with a card index is to use it. The information that a card provides will be similar to that of an on-line system (i.e. title and date of publication; author and publisher; shelf number).

Imagine having to search a large library for a book on English Language without a Catalogue.

The Dewey classification system

In Britain the most common classification system for publications is called the Dewey system (now the Universal Decimal Classification). In this system, each subject is allocated a number as follows:

000 GENERAL WORKS

100 PHILOSOPHY

200 RELIGION

300 SOCIAL SCIENCES

400 LANGUAGE

500 PURE SCIENCES

600 TECHNOLOGY (APPLIED SCIENCES)

700 THE ARTS

800 LITERATURE

900 HISTORY, GEOGRAPHY, BIOGRAPHY

Within each broad classification, there are more detailed subject divisions. For example:

600 TECHNOLOGY (APPLIED SCIENCES)

    610 MEDICAL SCIENCE
    620 ENGINEERING
    630 AGRICULTURE, FOOD PRODUCTION
    640 HOME ECONOMICS, HOUSECRAFT
    650 BUSINESS AND BUSINESS METHODS
    660 CHEMICAL TECHNOLOGY
    670 PROCESSING TRADES
    680 CRAFT TRADES
    690 BUILDING

Within each of these classifications there are further, more precise, breakdowns – for example, 643.7 classifies books on do-it-yourself activities.

Journals

Journals are also classified using the Dewey system. For example, at J658 you will find management journals. If you wish to research a particular topic, it may be necessary to consult an indexing journal (which lists articles, by subject, in a number of journals) or an abstracting journal (which gives a summary – or 'abstract' – of articles in a number of journals) in order to find out which journals to read.

Floorplans

Each library has a floorplan to show which shelves hold which classifications. All you have to do is go to the appropriate shelf to find the publication you want.

Using CD-ROM

Compact Disc Read-Only Memory (CD-ROM) is a computer disc that can store vast amounts of information and make it readily accessible to readers. Large reference works (such as dictionaries, encyclopedias, technical manuals), databases of

articles from books, newspapers and journals, and directories (such as information about companies and marketing) are all available on CD-ROM.

CD-ROM enables users to print out information, and to retrieve information and store it on a floppy disk.

Specialist databases

In addition to general databases, some libraries may have access to specialist databases, such as Datastream, which gives access to company accounts and share information.

Interlibrary loans

If you can't find the information you need in your library, it is possible (for a small charge) to request that the book or article be transferred from another library, through the interlibrary loan system. The librarians will have details.

Using reference books

All libraries stock a range of reference books, containing a wealth of useful information. They cannot usually be borrowed, but are intended to be dipped into for information. Consult a:

Dictionary – for definitions of words, examples of their use, pronunciation

Subject dictionary – for definitions of words relevant to a particular subject (e.g. Business, Electronics, Environment, Information Technology)

Thesaurus – for alternative words from which to choose

Encyclopedia – for brief information about any subject

There are many other reference works, e.g. to specific subjects; local businesses; government statistics; countries of the world.

The use of suitable reference books can be a quick and efficient way of gathering information, and can prepare the ground for more detailed study of other books on a subject.

It is sometimes necessary to consult more than one reference to clarify the meaning of a word or phrase. For example, if you are going abroad and a leaflet recommends that you be vaccinated against yellow fever and you wish to know a little about the disease,

a dictionary may tell you very little (e.g. yellow fever = tropical viral disease with fever and jaundice). If you want to know a little more it would be a good idea to consult a general encyclopedia, where you will discover that yellow fever is carried by the Stegomyia mosquito found in South and Central America and African ports. If you want a lot more information it will be necessary to consult a medical dictionary or other medical text.

Using telephone directories

Like other books, most telephone directories have a Table of Contents at the front, and some have a Classification Index at the back to help readers use the directory efficiently. For example, if you wish to discover which shops in your area can sell you a CD-ROM system, it may be necessary to consult the Classification Index for suitable sections of the *Yellow Pages* (e.g. Computers: peripherals, or alternatively, Audio Dealers: TV, Video & Radio Shops).

Mining a Book.

Mining books for information

Once you have found books or any other written materials that seem likely to contain the information you seek, you may be tempted to read them from beginning to end. This is time-consuming and often unnecessary. Reading is not a one-gear activity. Novels are usually read from cover to cover and fairly slowly – sometimes we don't want them to end. Poetry is sometimes read even more intensively, and the reader may ponder meaning, word use and rhythm. For the purposes of most communication, however, you need only extract or 'mine' the information and ideas that you seek. To do this it helps to have a clear question or focus in mind when reading.

 STOP AND THINK
How many reading gears do you have? Can you find the information you seek quickly? Do you need more practice in scanning and skimming?

Scanning, skimming, studying

The parts of a book that are likely to give you a quick overview of what it contains are the *Contents* page, the *Index* (at the back of the book) and, if the book has them, the *Summaries* (at the beginning or end of chapters).

All of these will give you clues about where to dip into the book for suitable material. Often the beginnings of chapters contain strong clues to what follows; and the ends of chapters often summarise what has gone before.

You can also scan through whole books, or whole chapters, allowing your eyes to take in large blocks of print, searching for the clues to relevant material. Then you can skim a number of pages, reading superficially, extracting only the main points. It is not necessary to always read forwards in a book or article – sometimes you will need to move backwards and forwards until you find what you are looking for.

Once you have found particular passages that are of interest to you, you may slow down to study the material, by reading it at a slower pace and perhaps making a few notes (see *Making notes*). If when reading you come across a term that you don't understand, you will find that the context often provides clues to meaning. Don't try to read text very closely, or stumble over individual words and sentences. Read quite quickly, ignore some of the detail and see how the main argument shapes. In this way, many words or phrases that may at first seem difficult will become clearer.

When you come across an unfamiliar word, the Index may show where else in the book the word is used and, by looking at its use several times, it is possible to work out the meaning, without needing to seek further clarification.

In this way you can mine many books in a short time, discarding books that seem irrelevant to your needs, and quickly extracting the information you need from others.

Understanding the subject

Often, when you read through written material for information or ideas you will already have some knowledge about the subject and what you are looking for. Identifying the main points or following the line of argument may, therefore, be relatively easy. However, sometimes you will need to read material with which you are not familiar; or to read material that is so complex that you will need help to understand it.

Some clarification of the main points can be gained from reading with care, making some notes, and consulting a dictionary or other reference work when necessary. In addition, you will find that it is sometimes necessary to consult other people. Some people find it difficult to ask another person for help. They feel it is like an admission of weakness. It is not. As the great scientist, Isaac Newton said, 'If I have seen far, it is by standing on the shoulders of giants'. Today you may seek help from another person, tomorrow it may be you who is asked for help.

Another means of clarification is simply to leave the apparent difficulty for a while. Do something else, and return to it afresh at another time. Very often the difficulty will have vanished – it was only tiredness or over-familiarity that led to you not seeing the obvious.

Reading, like speaking, listening and writing is not carried out by the mind alone. Our hearts and souls are also involved. For example, if someone writes you a letter of complaint that is less than tactfully expressed, you may feel a sense of hurt pride – 'How dare they' – that gets in the way of taking in the main points the letter makes. It is impossible to switch off our feelings completely when reading, but it is possible to be aware that our feelings can sometimes get in the way of understanding. If you find you are reacting emotionally to something, a cooling-off period before you reply is often a good idea.

 STOP AND THINK
Do you sometimes react too hastily when it would be wiser to consider your reply?

Making notes

Whether you are reading, preparing to speak or write, or recording what has been agreed, you will often need to make notes.

Here are some hints for making useful notes:

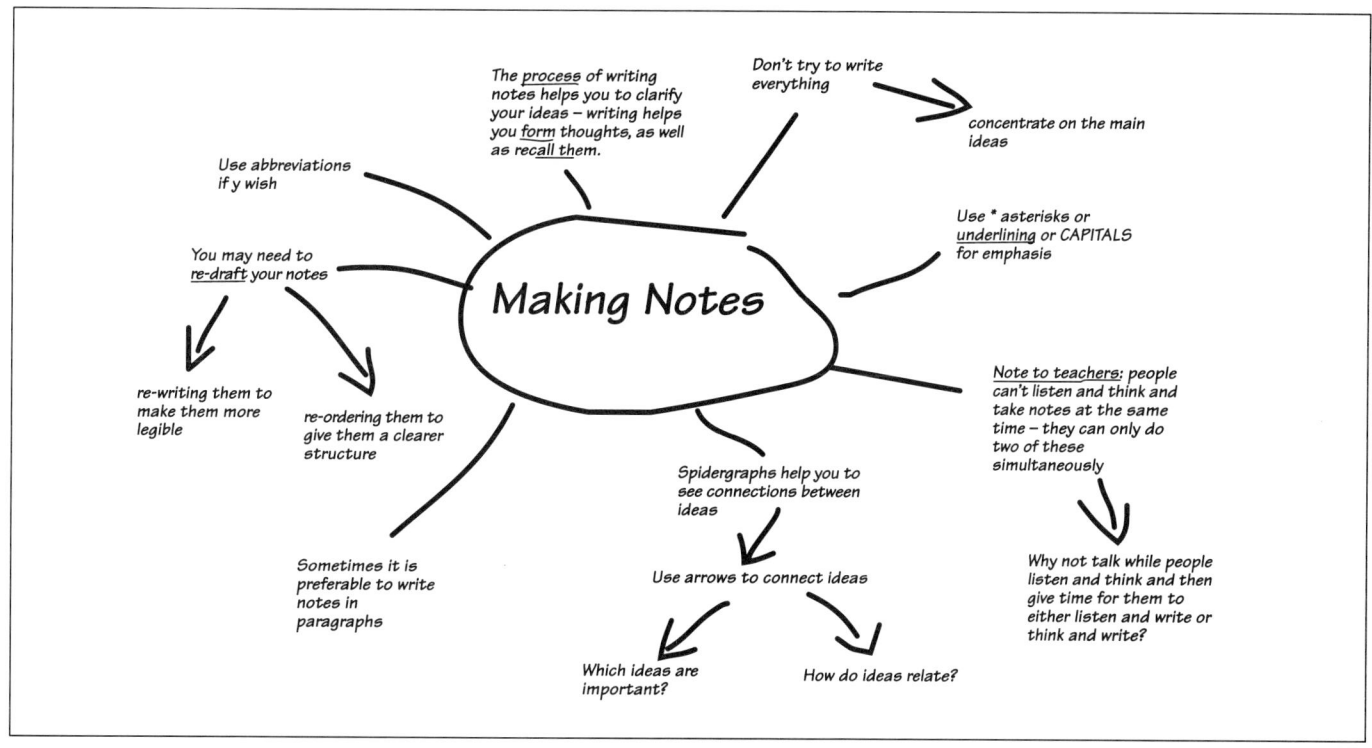

Making notes from a book

In order to summarise the information from books, it is helpful to use index cards that can be stored in a file box when making notes based on reading a book.

If there is any likelihood that you will quote from a book, or list it in a bibliography or reference section, be sure to record the author, year of publication, title and publisher at the top of the first card like this:

> Robinson, Peter (1995) Information
> Technology for Service GNVQs, Collins
> Educational.

Avoid the temptation to make lengthy summary notes. It is time-consuming and the result may be a dense mass of writing more difficult to read than the book itself. Summarising information involves identifying the main points from the extracted material and presenting them in a concise form, either orally or in writing.

It is very inconsiderate to mark a book that other people will use. However, if you feel you must write in the book itself, write in light pencil in the margin by anything you think may be noteworthy. Go back from time to time (e.g. after a chapter) to look again at what you have marked. Sometimes it will no longer seem worth noting, perhaps because there is a better statement later. If it is noteworthy make

brief notes, using abbreviations if you wish (usg abbrev if y wsh).

Remember to record accurately any words you might want to quote, and make a page reference.

If you don't own the book, rub out the light pencil. <u>Never</u> mark a book in ink. This will ruin it for future use.

 STOP AND THINK
How efficiently do you make notes? Do you read material without making sufficient notes? Are you a dreaded bookmarker who ruins books for other readers?

Avoid the temptation to make lengthy notes.

	Position in newspaper	Total number of words (approx)	Direct quotes from Rowntree report (no. of words)	Explanatory images
Daily Mail (tends to support Conservative)	p. 15	700	160	0
Daily Mirror (tends to support Labour)	pp. 6 and 7	1000	219	2
The Guardian (tends to support Labour/Liberal)	p. 1 and p. 15	1400	236	3
The Sun (tends to support Conservative)	p. 6	80 (but not directly about Rowntree report)	0	0

Judging the relevance of materials

Book and articles are written by human beings, all of whom are fallible. People express opinions and ideas which may or may not be correct, and they interpret facts according to particular standpoints of culture, circumstance and politics. When researching a topic it is sometimes necessary to read a range of materials in order to obtain a balanced view. This is especially the case when reading newspapers, most of which tend towards one political party.

The writers of books, articles and newspapers may put a bias on information they present by, for example:

- giving excessive prominence to facts and opinions that they agree with;

- ignoring facts and opinions that they disagree with;

- including facts and opinions that they disagree with but, consciously or subconsciously, misrepresenting them, either directly or by the use of biased language. One paper's 'peace initiative' may be another's 'propaganda ploy'; one political party may 'win' seats while another 'grabs' them; the same people may be called 'freedom fighters' or 'terrorists'. People who hold different views to the paper's may simply be dismissed as 'loonies', without any attempt to present their ideas;

- including facts and opinions that they disagree with but giving them little prominence;

- using photographs that have been trimmed or angled to show only what the paper wishes. For example, a few days before a general election, one paper showed a Labour leader addressing a public meeting attended apparently by only children. The rest of the audience had been cut out of the photograph.

(Examples taken from Keane, 1991)

Consider the coverage on 10 February 1995 by four national newspapers of a major report by the Rowntree Trust on Income and Wealth in Britain (see table above).

 STOP AND THINK
Do you read a newspaper? Which political party does it tend to support and how does this affect its coverage of news?

When researching a topic it is sometimes preferable to go to primary sources (i.e. to the actual report or research, rather than to second-hand accounts). However, this is often impracticable – the primary sources may not be available; you may not have time to consult them; they may be written for a specialist audience and not be understandable by other readers.

In practice, we have to rely on the accuracy and honesty of much that we read, but we should avoid thinking of printed text as embodying sacred wisdom – it rarely does, but instead presents the opinions and interpretations of fallible human beings. To compensate for this, it is wise to consult a range of materials in order to judge their relevance.